0 es

hamlyn | **all colour cookbook**

200 low fat dishes

Cara Hobday

An Hachette UK company

First published in Great Britain in 2008 by Hamlyn,
a division of Octopus Publishing Group Ltd
Endeavour House, 189 Shaftesbury Avenue,
London WC2H 8JY
www.octopusbooks.co.uk

Copyright © Octopus Publishing Group Ltd 2008

Some of the recipes in this book have previously
appeared in other books published by Hamlyn.

ISBN: 978-0-600-61732-7

A CIP catalogue record for this book is available from
the British Library

Printed and bound in China

3 4 5 6 7 8 9 10

All recipes contain 12 g of fat per serving or less (not
including serving suggestions)

Both metric and imperial measurements are given in all
recipes. Use one set of measurements, not a mix of both.

Standard level spoon measurements are used in all recipes:
1 tablespoon = one 15 ml spoon
1 teaspoon = one 5 ml spoon

Ovens should be preheated to the specified temperature
– if using a fan-assisted oven, follow the manufacturer's
instructions for adjusting the time and the temperature.

Fresh herbs should be used unless otherwise stated.

Medium eggs should be used unless otherwise stated.

The Department of Health advises that eggs should not be
eaten raw. This book contains some dishes made with raw
or lightly cooked eggs. It is prudent for vulnerable people
such as pregnant and nursing mothers, invalids, the elderly,
babies and young children to avoid uncooked or lightly
cooked dishes made with eggs. Once prepared, these
dishes should be kept refrigerated and used promptly.

This book includes dishes made with nuts and nut
derivatives. It is advisable for those with known allergic
reactions to nuts and nut derivatives and those who may
be potentially vulnerable to these allergies, such as
pregnant and nursing mothers, invalids, the elderly, babies
and children, to avoid dishes made with nuts and nut oils
and to check the labels of pre-prepared ingredients.

contents

introduction

introduction

We all know that we need to take care with what we eat. In the long term, sticking to a healthy diet requires us to look beyond the celebrity diets and weight-loss programmes. These may help lose a few pounds in the short term, but will not give a foundation for lasting healthy habits.

Changing habits

The most important change we can make is to reduce the amount of fat we consume. Eliminating all fat is unrealistic and in fact unhealthy, because fat is essential in the supply of vitamins A, D, E and K and for the production of new cells and hormones. However, permanently lowering the amount of fat in our diet should be the aim of all of us.

There is no shortage of advice about what constitutes a low-fat diet, and books

and magazines are full of articles about good fats versus bad fats, foods to avoid, cooking methods to use and even what size plate to put it all on. For most of us, putting this advice into practice is difficult. Translating the wealth of information into day-to-day cooking and changing the habits of a lifetime needs something more than a couple of paragraphs of nutritional science.

Going low fat

How can you reduce the amount of fat in your diet? What does it mean to make healthy choices? The recipes in this book will help to translate all the confusing advice into real food and well-balanced meals.

Following a reduced-fat diet does require a change in attitudes at the outset. Eating healthily means looking in a new way at how you shop and eat. Your aim is regular, well-balanced meals that contain enough starchy foods, vegetables and protein — a third of each on the plate is a good guide. Nutritious meals will take away the desire for unhealthy, fat-rich snacks in between.

Cooking for a family can be difficult, as you have to satisfy a range of different needs and tastes. Try sitting down with your family and selecting a few recipes from this book to sample. Remember that most recipes can be simplified for small children and toddlers.

Shopping for low-fat cooking

Making a list before you shop will help you to walk past the high-fat ready meals and ignore snacks and sweets. Many ingredients are available in healthier versions. Full-fat dairy products, for example, are easily substituted for the low-fat versions: choose skimmed or semi-skimmed milk instead of full-fat milk and fat-free or reduced-fat yogurt instead of full-milk products. If you select extra thick single cream you won't miss double cream. Sunflower spread can be used instead of butter in most types of baking.

Look again at the amazing array of fruit and vegetables available. Experiment with new salad leaves and have fun with fruit. Pineapples and mangoes contain just as much vitamin C as oranges and kiwifruit. Although buying locally produced, in-season fruit and vegetables is the ideal, the freezer section of your supermarket will also offer more unusual items to tempt the family. Soy beans, baby broad beans and sweetcorn freeze well, and frozen fruits, such as raspberries and blueberries, are wonderful in winter puddings.

The meat counter offers some healthy alternatives. Pork can be one of the leanest cuts available if you choose fillets and not pork belly. Lean pork mince is also widely available, or you could buy fillet and mince it

yourself. If you prefer lamb, look out for leg steaks rather than the fattier chops.

Chicken breast is the leanest part of the bird, and you can reduce the fat content still further by buying skinless cuts or removing the skin yourself. Turkey is also a low-fat option, so consider replacing the ham in your lunchbox sandwiches with cold cooked turkey.

Don't forget to buy healthy cooking oil. An oil spray will transform pan-fried meals into low-fat versions. If you cannot find a spray, wipe away excess oil from your frying pan with kitchen paper before frying onions or garlic.

Another easy way to reduce your intake of saturated fat is to eat fish instead of meat two or three times a week. Supermarkets often have excellent fish counters, and frozen

enables you to dry-fry foods without fear of them sticking, although bear in mind that the temperature for dry-frying has to be just right: too low, and the food sticks to the pan; too high, and it will burn without cooking. You will need nonstick utensils to protect the surface of the pan.

A chargrill pan allows you to transform a simple fish fillet into a Mediterranean delight. It will also cook chops and other cuts of meat while letting the fat drain away. Make sure the pan is really hot: allow about 10 minutes to preheat the pan. Buy a heavy pan that will hold the heat well. Operating on the same principle — but easier to clean — are the low-fat grilling machines. All types enable cooking while draining excess fat away.

fish is widely available. A simple fresh fish fillet, seasoned and quickly grilled, is the basis of a delicious and healthy meal.

Ready-made cakes and biscuits contain a lot of fat — often the 'wrong' kind. Walk straight past the biscuits and on to the home baking section. Although your home-baked cakes and biscuits will contain some fat, you can control the type and choose sunflower and low-fat spreads.

Equipment

A steamer is a good investment if you are aiming to reduce your fat intake. Steamers quickly and cleanly cook several things at a time and all over a single heat source. You will find that steamed vegetables have such a great flavour that you will not miss the salt, and none of the goodness is lost in the water.

A large, good-quality, nonstick frying pan or wok with a lid is invaluable. A nonstick pan

Methods

If you regularly fry foods ask yourself if they can be grilled or roasted instead. Set your lamb chop or steak on a grill rack and the fat will drain off into the roasting tray below. Grilling or roasting also makes it easier to add flavours. For example, you can top a piece of salmon with lemon slices or add some chopped herbs to the basting juices of chicken fillets.

Deep-fried vegetables can often be baked. For healthier chips, toss potato chips or wedges in a little oil and seasoning and bake in a preheated oven, 200°C (400°F), Gas Mark 6, for about 20 minutes.

Plan ahead and make casseroles and stews the day before. If you leave them overnight in the refrigerator, the flavour will improve and the fat will solidify at the surface so that you can easily skim it off.

Serving suggestions

When you serve your delicious, well-balanced, low-fat meal, you can make it even more appealing with a few tweaks at the table. Changing the size of serving plates is often cited as a good place to start if you want to reduce your overall intake of calories. A medium-sized portion on a small plate will look more filling than the same portion on a large plate.

If you like to add butter to baked potatoes, try offering Greek yogurt instead. Instead of serving bread with butter, simply offer it without butter or with oil to dip into. If you spread jam on hot toast you will not miss the butter. A tasty raspberry coulis, widely available from supermarkets, will be better for you and your family than a spoonful of double cream on a fresh fruit salad.

Rather than offering ready-made mayonnaise try a range of relishes or chutneys. Mango chutney goes happily with many recipes and lime pickle is an excellent accompaniment for salmon. Use tomato relish to pep up your burgers.

The key to low-fat cooking and eating is to include lots of flavour to replace the richness of the fat. Serve interesting vegetables and the absence of a creamy sauce will be unremarked. Try unusual combinations, such as courgettes and red pepper, runner beans and green beans, to tempt jaded taste buds. Toss baked peppers through steamed potatoes, or try finishing off steamed vegetables with chopped chives and parsley and a little grated lemon.

Once you have started to change your habits, you will not regret the decision to cook and eat a lower fat diet. When you take in unnecessary extra fat, your body has to expend energy to process and store it. As soon as you reduce your fat intake, you will immediately feel the difference in your energy levels. And more energy means that you can be more active, thereby further improving your overall health.

Enjoy the recipes in this book, and may your low fat regime last.

everyday

spicy pork, fried rice & greens

Serves **4**
Preparation time **15 minutes**,
   plus marinating
Cooking time **20 minutes**

200 g (7 oz) **easy-cook
   basmati rice**
3 tablespoons **hoisin sauce**
2 **garlic cloves**, crushed
5 cm (2 inch) piece **fresh root
   ginger**, grated
1 **red chilli**, sliced
1 **star anise**
1 tablespoon **sun-dried
   tomato purée**
300 g (10 oz) **pork fillet**, cut
   into thin strips
sunflower oil spray
1 **red onion**, chopped
125 g (4 oz) **cabbage** or
   spring greens, finely
   chopped
1 **carrot**, finely sliced
toasted sesame seeds,
   to serve

Cook the rice in boiling salted water for 16–18 minutes. Drain and set aside.

Meanwhile, mix together the hoisin sauce, garlic, ginger, chilli, star anise and tomato purée. Toss the pork in the mixture, cover and set aside for up to 1 hour.

Heat a wok over high heat and spray with oil. Remove the pork from the marinade (discard the remainder) and cook the meat in the wok for about 1 minute. Stir in the onion, cabbage and carrot, then the rice. Toss and stir everything together over high heat for about 3 minutes, until the rice is hot. Sprinkle with sesame seeds and serve.

For hoisin lamb with stir-fry noodles, use 300 g (10 oz) lamb fillet instead of pork and omit the rice and tomato purée. Marinate and stir-fry the lamb with the vegetables as above. Then add 3 x 150 g (5 oz) packets straight-to-wok rice noodles (or dried rice noodles, cooked according to the packet instructions) and stir-fry for about 1 minute, until hot. Sprinkle with chopped fresh coriander leaves instead of sesame seeds and serve.

chicken satay

Serves **4**
Preparation time **10 minutes**,
   plus marinating
Cooking time **10 minutes**

25 g (1 oz) **smooth peanut
   butter**
125 ml (4 fl oz) **soy sauce**
125 ml (4 fl oz) **lime juice**
15 g (½ oz) **curry powder**
2 **garlic cloves**, chopped
1 teaspoon **hot pepper sauce**
6 boneless, skinless **chicken
   breasts**, about 125 g
   (4 oz) each, cubed

Presoak 12 wooden skewers in warm water. Mix
together the peanut butter, soy sauce, lime juice, curry
powder, garlic and hot pepper sauce in a large bowl.

Put the chicken in the marinade and leave to marinate
in the refrigerator for about 8 hours or overnight.

Thread the chicken onto skewers and transfer to a
foil-lined grill pan. Cook under a preheated hot grill for
5 minutes on each side.

For pork satay, marinate cubed pork in a mixture of
3 crushed garlic cloves, ½ teaspoon each ground
cumin and ground cinnamon, 1 teaspoon each ground
coriander and turmeric, 2 teaspoons caster sugar,
2 tablespoons lime juice, 4 finely sliced spring onions
and 2 tablespoons olive oil. Thread onto skewers and
cook as above.

chicken with lemon & parsley

Serves **4**
Preparation time **5 minutes**
Cooking time **8 minutes**

4 boneless, skinless **chicken breasts**, about 125 g (4 oz) each
1 tablespoon **olive oil**
25 g (1 oz) **butter**
2 tablespoons **lemon juice**
3 tablespoons chopped **parsley**
1 tablespoon chopped **oregano**
salt and pepper
lemon wedges, to serve

Use a sharp knife to cut each chicken breast in half horizontally. Transfer the chicken to a foil-lined grill pan and season.

Put the oil, butter, lemon juice, parsley and oregano in a small pan and heat until the butter is melted. Spoon or brush this mix over the chicken.

Grill the chicken in batches under a preheated hot grill for about 4 minutes until just cooked and still succulent. Serve immediately with lemon wedges and, if liked, wholewheat pasta.

For spicy chicken salad wraps, add a deseeded chopped red chilli to the mixture with the parsley and oregano and grill as above. Warm 8 wheat tortillas in the bottom of the grill compartment while cooking the chicken. Mix 150 g (5 oz) each watercress and rocket and divide among the tortillas. Slice the chicken thinly and arrange on the leaves, then roll up and serve with lemon wedges.

beef & pepper kebabs

Serves **4**
Preparation time **15 minutes**,
  plus marinating
Cooking time **15 minutes**

400 g (13 oz) **steak**, rump
  or topside
1 **red pepper**, cored and
  deseeded
1 **green pepper**, cored and
  deseeded
1 teaspoon crushed **coriander
  seeds**
3 tablespoons **vegetable oil**
15 g (½ oz) chopped **fresh
  coriander**
1 **red chilli**, deseeded and
  chopped
1 **garlic clove**, crushed
2 tablespoons **lime juice**
4 **chapattis**
salt and pepper

Presoak 8 wooden skewers in warm water. Cut the beef and peppers into 2.5 cm (1 inch) cubes.

Mix together the coriander seeds, 2 tablespoons oil and half the chopped coriander in a bowl and season to taste. Add the beef and peppers and toss to coat.

Thread the beef and peppers on to the skewers, cover and refrigerate for up to 1 hour.

Mix together the remaining coriander and oil with the chilli, garlic and lime juice to make a dressing, season to taste and set aside.

Grill the skewers under a preheated hot grill for 15 minutes, turning often and basting with the juices. Warm the chapattis under the grill.

Serve 2 skewers per person on a hot chapatti and drizzle over the coriander dressing.

For lime & chive couscous, to serve as an accompaniment, put 250 g (8 oz) couscous in a bowl and pour on enough boiling water to cover it by 2.5 cm (1 inch). Cover the bowl and leave to stand for about 5 minutes, until the water is absorbed and the couscous is plump. Stir in the grated rind and juice of 1 lime and 3 tablespoons snipped fresh chives. Serve topped with the kebabs and the coriander dressing.

haddock parcels & coconut rice

Serves **4**
Preparation time **15 minutes**
Cooking time **20 minutes**

4 **haddock fillets**, about
  150 g (5 oz) each
4 tablespoons chopped **fresh
  coriander**
1 **red chilli**, chopped
1 **shallot**, finely sliced
1 **lime**, sliced, plus extra lime
  halves to serve
2 **lemon grass stalks**,
  1 roughly chopped and
  1 bashed
200 g (7 oz) **Thai jasmine
  rice**
2 fresh or dried **kaffir lime
  leaves**
50 ml (2 fl oz) **reduced-fat
  coconut milk**

Cut 4 pieces of nonstick baking paper, each 30 cm
(12 inches) square. Put a haddock fillet in the centre
of each piece and arrange some of the coriander, chilli,
shallot, lime and chopped lemon grass stalk evenly over
each. Wrap them up into neat parcels.

Transfer the parcels to a baking sheet and cook in
a preheated oven, 180°C (350°F), Gas Mark 4, for
20 minutes.

Meanwhile, put the rice in a pan with 400 ml (14 fl oz)
water, the bashed lemon grass stalk and the lime
leaves. Cover and simmer for 12 minutes. When the
rice is cooked and the water absorbed, stir in the
coconut milk. Serve with the haddock parcels, with
some extra lime halves.

For salmon parcels with sesame rice, use 150 g
(5 oz) portions of skinless salmon fillet instead of the
haddock. Use lemon slices instead of lime and omit
the lemon grass. Sprinkle a few drops of sesame oil
over each salmon portion and cook as above. Omit
the lime leaves and coconut milk from the rice. Fork
2 tablespoons toasted sesame seeds and 2 chopped
spring onions into the cooked rice and serve with the
salmon, adding lemon wedges for additional zest.

blackened salmon with salsa

Serves **4**
Preparation time **15 minutes**
Cooking time **8 minutes**

3 tablespoons **Cajun
  seasoning**
1 teaspoon **dried oregano**
4 **salmon fillets**, about 75 g
  (3 oz) each
sunflower oil, to brush
lime wedges, to garnish

Cajun salsa
410 g (13½ oz) can **black-
  eyed beans**, rinsed and
  drained
2 tablespoons **olive oil**
1 **avocado**, peeled, stoned
  and chopped
2 **plum tomatoes**, finely
  chopped
1 **yellow pepper**, deseeded
  and finely chopped
2 tablespoons **lime juice**
salt and pepper

Mix together the Cajun seasoning and oregano in a shallow bowl.

Brush the salmon on both sides with a little oil and coat with the spice mix, making sure the fish is completely covered. Set aside.

Meanwhile, make the salsa by mixing together all the ingredients in a bowl. Season to taste and set aside.

Cook the salmon in a preheated, dry frying pan for 4 minutes on each side.

Slice the salmon and serve with the salsa, with lime wedges to garnish.

For salsa verde, drain and finely chop 6 anchovy fillets in oil and combine them with 3 tablespoons chopped basil, 3 tablespoons chopped parsley or chives, 2 teaspoons roughly chopped capers, 2 teaspoons Dijon mustard, 3 tablespoons olive oil and 1½ tablespoons white wine vinegar.

prawn skewers with relish

Serves **4**
Preparation time **10 minutes**
Cooking time **10 minutes**

50 g (2 oz) **gherkins**, finely
   chopped
50 g (2 oz) **cucumber**, finely
   chopped
1 **shallot**, finely chopped
50 ml (2 fl oz) **olive oil**
1½ tablespoons **white wine
   vinegar**
1 tablespoon roughly
   chopped **dill**
400 g (13 oz) raw **tiger
   prawns**
salt and pepper

Presoak 12 wooden skewers in warm water. Mix
together the gherkins, cucumber and shallot in a small
dish. In a separate bowl mix together the oil, vinegar
and dill and season to taste.

Thread about 4 prawns on to each skewer and cook
under a preheated hot grill for about 10 minutes, turning
once or twice, until the prawns are cooked through.

Arrange the prawn skewers on 4 plates. Pour the
dressing over the gherkin mixture and stir to mix.
Spoon the relish over the prawns and serve with new
potatoes, if liked.

**For scallop skewers with cucumber & avocado
relish**, use 16 small scallops without roes instead of
the prawns. Halve, stone, peel and dice 2 firm but ripe
avocados and mix them with the cucumber, omitting
the gherkins. Dress the relish as soon as the avocado
is diced. Brush the scallops very lightly with a little
olive oil and grill for 2–3 minutes on each side, until
just firm and opaque. Serve the scallops and relish
with new potatoes or rice.

plaice with herby coconut crust

Serves **4**
Preparation time **10 minutes**
Cooking time **15 minutes**

30 g (1½ oz) **desiccated coconut**
50 g (2 oz) **breadcrumbs**
2 tablespoons chopped **chives**
pinch of **paprika**
4 **skinless plaice fillets**
salt and pepper
lime wedges, to serve

Mix together the coconut, breadcrumbs, chives and paprika and season to taste.

Arrange the fish fillets on a baking sheet, top each one with some of the coconut mixture and cook in a preheated oven, 180°C (350°F), Gas Mark 4, for 15 minutes.

Serve the fish with lime wedges and accompanied with baked potatoes and a rocket salad, if liked.

For lemon sole with an almond crust, substitute the plaice fillets for 4 skinless lemon sole fillets. In the topping, use 50 g (2 oz) flaked almonds instead of coconut. Serve the fish with new potatoes, watercress and lemon wedges.

penne with roasted tomatoes

Serves **4**
Preparation time **15 minutes**
Cooking time **15 minutes**

500 g (1 lb) **cherry tomatoes**,
   halved
2 tablespoons **olive oil**
2 **garlic cloves**, finely
   chopped
4–5 stems of **rosemary**
large pinch of **paprika** or
   chilli powder
375 g (12 oz) dried
   wholewheat penne
2 tablespoons **balsamic
   vinegar**
4 tablespoons **low-fat crème
   fraîche** or **ricotta**
salt and pepper
Parmesan cheese shavings,
   to serve

Put the tomatoes in a roasting tin, drizzle over the oil and sprinkle with the garlic, the torn leaves from 3 rosemary stems, paprika or chilli powder and a little seasoning. Cook in a preheated oven, 200°C (400°F), Gas Mark 6, for 15 minutes or until just softened.

Meanwhile, cook the pasta in a large saucepan of boiling water for 10–12 minutes or until just tender, then drain.

Spoon the balsamic vinegar into the tomatoes, add the drained pasta and crème fraîche or ricotta and toss together. Spoon the penne into bowls and top with Parmesan shavings.

For penne with tomatoes, pine nuts & raisins, omit the paprika or chilli powder and add a handful each of pine nuts and raisins to the roasting tin, then proceed as above. Serve scattered with diced mozzarella rather than Parmesan and allow the cheese to soften before serving.

lamb & prune tagine with barley

Serves **4**
Preparation time **15 minutes**
Cooking time **1–1¼ hours**

olive oil spray
625 g (1¼ lb) lean diced **lamb**
1 **red onion**, chopped
1 **carrot**, peeled and chopped
1 teaspoon **paprika**
1 teaspoon **ground coriander**
1 teaspoon **fennel seeds**
3 cm (1¼ inch) **cinnamon stick**
2 **garlic cloves**, crushed
2 **bay leaves**
2 tablespoons **lime juice**
750 ml (1¼ pints) **chicken stock**
75 g (3 oz) **dried prunes**
400 g (13 oz) can **chopped tomatoes**
65 g (2½ oz) **pearl barley**
15 g (½ oz) chopped **fresh coriander,** plus extra sprigs to garnish
1 tablespoon **lime juice**
400 g (13 oz) **couscous**
salt and pepper

Heat a large saucepan or 2 litre (3½ pint) flameproof casserole, spray lightly with oil and cook the lamb briefly, in batches if necessary, until brown. Remove the lamb with a slotted spoon, add the onion and carrot to the pan and cook briefly to brown. Return the lamb, stir in all the remaining ingredients and season to taste.

Simmer covered for 1 hour or until the lamb is tender. At the end of the cooking time, stir in the coriander and lime juice.

Meanwhile, cook the couscous according to the instructions on the packet and set aside for 5 minutes. Serve the hot tagine over the couscous and garnish with coriander sprigs.

For pork & apricot tagine, replace the lamb with the same quantity of diced pork and substitute the dried prunes for dried apricots. Toast a generous handful of split almonds in a dry pan over a medium heat, then stir into the casserole along with the other ingredients.

turkey burgers & sweet potatoes

Serves **4**
Preparation time **15 minutes**,
  plus chilling
Cooking time **40 minutes**

750 g (1½ lb) **sweet
  potatoes**, washed but
  unpeeled and cut into
  wedges
2 tablespoons **sunflower oil**
500 g (1 lb) **turkey mince**
½ **red pepper**, cored,
  deseeded and chopped
325 g (11 oz) can **sweetcorn**,
  rinsed and drained
1 **onion**, chopped
1 **egg**, beaten
6 **wholemeal bread rolls**
salt and pepper

Toss the potato wedges in 1 tablespoon oil, season to taste and bake in a preheated oven, 200°C (400°F), Gas Mark 6, for 30 minutes, turning after 15 minutes.

Meanwhile, in a large bowl mix together the mince with the red pepper, sweetcorn and onion. Season to taste and add the egg. Shape the mixture into 6 burgers and refrigerate until ready to cook.

Heat the remaining oil in a shallow frying pan over medium heat. Add the burgers, 3 at a time, and cook for 2 minutes on each side until brown. Transfer to a baking sheet and finish cooking in the oven, below the potato wedges, for 15 minutes or until cooked through.

Cut the rolls in half and cook them, cut side down, in the hot pan. Put a few salad leaves and tomato slices in each roll, add a burger and serve them with the sweet potato wedges.

For lamb & chickpea burgers, replace the turkey with 300 g (10 oz) minced lamb. Take 2 x 400 g (13 oz) cans chickpeas and mash them roughly with a fork. When mixing all the ingredients, omit the sweetcorn and replace it with the mashed chickpeas.

chicken with red kidney beans

Serves **4**
Preparation time **15 minutes**
Cooking time **20–25 minutes**

sunflower oil spray
1 **onion**, roughly chopped
1 **red pepper**, cored,
　deseeded and roughly
　chopped
1 **garlic clove**, halved
250 g (8 oz) boneless,
　skinless **chicken thighs**, cut
　into 3 cm (1¼ inch) dice
2 teaspoons **mild chilli
　powder**
200 g (7 oz) **easy-cook
　long-grain rice**
410 g (13½ oz) can **red
　kidney beans**, rinsed and
　drained
395 g (12½ oz) can **cherry
　tomatoes in natural juice**
200 ml (7 fl oz) **chicken stock**
salt and pepper

To serve
fresh coriander leaves,
　roughly chopped
lime wedges

Heat a large frying pan with a flameproof handle and lightly spray with oil. Add the onion, red pepper, garlic and chicken and cook, stirring, over a medium heat for 3 minutes.

Add the chilli powder, rice, beans, tomatoes and stock to the pan, season to taste, bring to the boil and simmer for 15 minutes.

When the rice and chicken are cooked, spoon as much of the chicken on top of the rice as you can and cook under a preheated hot grill until golden.

Serve with chopped coriander and lime wedges.

For chicken & chickpea casserole, replace the kidney beans with a 410 g (13½ oz) can chickpeas and add ½ teaspoon ground cinnamon, the juice of ½ lemon and the other ingredients at the second stage. Omit the ground ginger and orange rind. Cook as above, then garnish with mint leaves rather than lime wedges.

chilli pork with pineapple rice

Serves **4**
Preparation time **20 minutes**,
  plus marinating
Cooking time **15 minutes**

2 tablespoons **sunflower oil**
2 tablespoons **lime juice**
2 **garlic cloves**, crushed
1 **red chilli**, deseeded and
  finely chopped
300 g (10 oz) **pork fillet**,
  cubed
200 g (7 oz) **Thai fragrant
  rice**
6 **spring onions**, finely sliced
200 g (7 oz) **pineapple**,
  peeled and diced
½ **red onion**, cut into wedges
1 **lime**, cut into wedges
salt and pepper
ready-made **sweet chilli
  sauce**, to serve

Presoak 8 wooden skewers in warm water. Mix together the oil, lime juice, garlic, chilli and salt and pepper in a bowl, add the pork and stir to coat. Cover and refrigerate for at least 1 hour.

Meanwhile, cook the rice in lightly salted boiling water for 12–15 minutes or according to the instructions on the packet. Drain and stir through the spring onions and pineapple.

Thread the pork on to the skewers, alternating it with onion and lime wedges, and cook under a preheated hot grill for about 10 minutes, turning frequently and basting with the remaining marinade, until the pork is cooked through.

Put the skewers and rice on a plate with the sweet chilli sauce and serve immediately.

For chilli gammon, replace the pork with 300 g (10 oz) cubed gammon and use 1 green pepper, cut into wedges, instead of the lime. When threading the gammon onto the skewers, alternate it with onion wedges and green pepper wedges. Serve with mango chutney instead of sweet chilli sauce.

quick

chicken noodle miso soup

Serves **4**

Preparation time **15 minutes**

Cooking time **20 minutes**

sunflower oil spray

5 cm (2 inch) piece **fresh root
  ginger,** peeled and chopped

3 **garlic cloves,** crushed

pinch of **crushed chillies**

3 tablespoons **miso paste**

2 tablespoons **lime juice**

200 g (7 oz) **fine egg
  noodles**

2 **chicken breasts,** 125 g
  (4 oz) each, finely sliced

125 g (4 oz) **shiitake
  mushrooms,** sliced

65 g (2½ oz) **baby sweetcorn,**
  chopped

200 g (7 oz) **sugar snap
  peas,** halved

85 g (3¼ oz) **watercress,**
  tough stems removed

soy sauce, to serve

Heat a large saucepan, spray the bottom with oil, add
the ginger, garlic and chillies and stir-fry for 1 minute.
Add 1.8 litres (3 pints) boiling water and bring to a
simmer. Stir in the miso paste, lime juice and noodles
and cook for 1 minute. Cover and set aside.

Heat a large wok or frying pan, spray it with oil and
stir-fry the chicken, mushrooms and sweetcorn for
2–3 minutes. Add the peas and cook for 2 minutes.

Transfer the soup to 4 bowls, spoon over the
vegetables and chicken and top with watercress.
Serve the soy sauce on the side.

For vegetable miso soup with shredded omelette,
omit the chicken and prepare 2 omelettes using
2 eggs and 2 sliced spring onions each. When the
omelettes are cooked, roll and shred them, then
spoon over the soup with the vegetables.

fresh broad bean & herb dip

Serves **4**
Preparation time **5 minutes**,
    plus chilling
Cooking time **15 minutes**

375 g (12 oz) fresh or frozen
    broad beans
50 g (2 oz) **parsley**, roughly
    chopped
50 g (2 oz) **fresh coriander**,
    roughly chopped
1–2 **green chillies**, deseeded
    and chopped
2 **garlic cloves**, chopped
1½ teaspoons **ground cumin**
3 tablespoons **olive oil**
1 **onion**, thinly sliced
salt and pepper

Cook the beans in lightly salted boiling water for
5 minutes. Add the parsley and coriander, cover and
simmer for a further 5 minutes. Strain and reserve
some of the cooking liquid.

Combine the beans with the chillies, garlic, cumin,
2 tablespoons oil and 3–4 tablespoons of the reserved
cooking liquid in a food processor or blender. Process
to a smooth paste and season to taste. Add a little
more of the cooking liquid if the mixture is too dry.
Transfer to a serving dish and chill.

Heat the rest of the oil in a nonstick pan and fry the
onion briskly until golden and crisp. Spread over the
dip. If liked, serve the dip with wholemeal pitta bread
or crudités.

For aubergine dip, bake 2 foil-wrapped aubergines in
a preheated oven, 180°C (350°F), Gas Mark 4, for
30–45 minutes. Mash the flesh with 2–3 crushed
garlic cloves, 2 tablespoons olive oil and 1 tablespoon
lemon juice. Season to taste.

grilled teriyaki bass with noodles

Serves **4**
Preparation time **5 minutes**
Cooking time **10 minutes**

sunflower oil spray
4 **bass fillets**, about 175 g
  (6 oz) each
250 g (8 oz) medium **egg
  noodles**
1 tablespoons **sesame oil**
2 tablespoons finely chopped
  chives
3 **spring onions**, finely
  chopped

Teriyaki sauce
75 ml (3 fl oz) **mirin** or
  medium dry sherry
75 ml (3 fl oz) **light soy sauce**
75 ml (3 fl oz) **chicken stock**

Make the teriyaki sauce. Put the mirin or sherry in a saucepan, bring to the boil and simmer for 2 minutes or until reduced by half. Add the soy sauce and stock, stir and remove from the heat.

Line a grill pan with foil, spray with oil and arrange the bass fillets on the foil. Brush the fish with the teriyaki sauce and cook under a preheated hot grill for 5–6 minutes, basting often with the sauce.

Meanwhile, cook the noodles in lightly salted boiling water for 3 minutes or according to the instructions on the packet. Drain and stir in the sesame oil, chives and spring onions.

Serve the bass on a bed of piping hot noodles and drizzle over any juices from the grill pan.

For teriyaki tofu with stir-fried cabbage, replace the bass with 2 x 250 g (8 oz) packets tofu. Slice horizontally and cook as above. Meanwhile, stir-fry 250 g (8 oz) shredded Chinese cabbage and 1 sliced red pepper. Serve the tofu hot on a bed of the stir-fried cabbage.

marinated minty lamb kebabs

Serves **4**
Preparation time **15 minutes**,
  plus marinating
Cooking time **10 minutes**

1 **garlic clove**, crushed
2 tablespoons chopped **mint**
1 tablespoon ready-made **mint
  sauce**
150 g (5 oz) **low-fat natural
  yogurt**
375 g (12 oz) **lean lamb**,
  cubed
2 small **onions**, cut into
  wedges
1 **green pepper**, cored,
  deseeded and cut into
  wedges
lemon wedges, to serve

Mix together the garlic, mint, mint sauce and yogurt in a medium bowl, add the lamb and stir well. Cover and leave to marinate in a cool place for 10 minutes.

Thread the lamb and onion and pepper wedges on to 8 metal skewers and cook under a preheated hot grill for 8—10 minutes or until cooked through.

Serve the kebabs with lemon wedges and, if liked, accompany them with a green salad and couscous.

For Chinese lamb kebabs, marinate the lamb in a mixture of 5 cm (2 inches) fresh root ginger, peeled and finely grated, 4 tablespoons each soy sauce and dry sherry, 1 teaspoon caster sugar and 1 tablespoon lemon juice. Grill as above.

tuna enchiladas

Serves **4**

Preparation time **10 minutes**

Cooking time **15 minutes**

2 ripe **tomatoes**

1 **red onion**, peeled and finely chopped

1 tablespoon **lime juice** or to taste

8 **chapattis**

300 g (10 oz) can **tuna in spring water**, drained

150 g (5 oz) **reduced-fat Cheddar cheese**, grated

salt and pepper

fresh coriander, chopped, to garnish

Chop the tomatoes and mix them with the onion. Season well and add lime juice to taste.

Spoon some of the tomato mixture over each chapatti, top with the tuna and half the cheese. Roll up each chapatti and arrange them in a heatproof dish. Sprinkle over the remaining cheese and any remaining tomato salsa.

Cover and cook in a preheated oven, 200°C (400°F), Gas Mark 6, for 15 minutes until golden. Garnish with coriander and serve immediately.

For veggie enchiladas, slice and grill 12 mushrooms and 2 courgettes and and use instead of the tuna. For extra spice, add a chopped and deseeded jalapeño pepper to the tomatoes and onions.

salmon & bulgar wheat pilaf

Serves **4**
Preparation time **10 minutes**
Cooking time **10–15 minutes**

475 g (15 oz) boneless,
  skinless **salmon**
250 g (8 oz) **bulgar wheat**
75 g (3 oz) frozen **peas**
200 g (7 oz) **runner beans**,
  chopped
2 tablespoons chopped
  chives
2 tablespoons chopped **flat
  leaf parsley**
salt and pepper

To serve
2 **lemons**, halved
low-fat yogurt

Cook the salmon in a steamer or microwave for about 10 minutes. Alternatively, wrap it in foil and cook in a preheated oven, 180°C (350°F), Gas Mark 4, for 15 minutes.

Meanwhile, cook the bulgar wheat according to the instructions on the packet and boil the peas and beans. Alternatively, cook the bulgar wheat, peas and beans in the steamer with the salmon.

Flake the salmon and mix it into the bulgar wheat with the peas and beans. Fold in the chives and parsley and season to taste. Serve immediately with lemon halves and yogurt.

For ham & bulgar wheat pilaf, pan-fry 300 g (10 oz) diced lean ham instead of the salmon. Replace the runner beans with the same quantity of broad beans and fold in 2 tablespoons chopped mint along with the chives and parsley.

lamb with hummus & tortillas

Serves **4**

Preparation time **30 minutes**, plus marinating

Cooking time **12 minutes**

500 g (1 lb) **lamb fillet**, cut into 15 mm (¾ inch) slices

grated rind and juice of
  1 **lemon**

1 sprig of **rosemary**, chopped

3 mixed **peppers**, cored, deseeded and chopped

1 small **aubergine**, sliced

4 flour **tortillas**

Hummus

410 g (13½ oz) can **chickpeas**, rinsed and drained

2 tablespoons **Greek yogurt**

2 tablespoons **lemon juice**

1 tablespoon chopped **parsley**

Put the lamb, lemon rind and juice, rosemary and peppers in a non-metallic bowl and stir well. Cover and leave to marinate in a cool place for 30 minutes.

Meanwhile, put the hummus ingredients in a food processor or blender and process for 30 seconds. Spoon into a bowl.

Heat a griddle or heavy-based frying pan, add the lamb and pepper mixture and the aubergine and fry for 3—4 minutes until cooked. (You may need to do this in batches.)

Heat the tortillas according to the instructions on the packet. When the lamb and vegetables are ready, wrap them in the tortillas with the hummus and serve with some rocket, if liked.

For roasted vegetables with hummus, cut the following vegetables into wedges: 1 aubergine, 1 red pepper, 2 courgettes and 1 red onion. Drizzle with olive oil and sprinkle over 1 teaspoon chopped thyme. Roast in a preheated oven, 200°C (400°F), Gas Mark 6, for 45 minutes. When the vegetables are tender, wrap them in warm tortillas with the hummus prepared as above.

pork with red pepper & noodles

Serves **4**
Preparation time **30 minutes**
Cooking time **10 minutes**

150 g (5 oz) **flat rice noodles**
sunflower oil spray
3 **spring onions**, sliced
1 **red pepper**, diced
2 **kaffir lime leaves**,
   shredded
2 **red chillies**, deseeded
   and sliced
½ **lemon grass stalk**, finely
   chopped
450 g (14½ oz) **pork fillet**,
   shredded
2 tablespoons **soy sauce**
1 tablespoon **Thai fish sauce**
2 teaspoons **palm sugar** or
   soft brown sugar

To garnish
red basil or **basil leaves**
shredded **spring onions**

Cook the noodles according to the instructions on the packet.

Heat a wok or large frying pan and lightly spray with oil. Add the spring onions, red pepper, lime leaves, chillies and lemon grass and stir-fry for 1 minute. Add the shredded pork and stir-fry over high heat for 2 minutes.

Add the soy sauce, fish sauce, sugar and drained noodles and cook for about 2 minutes, using 2 spoons to lift and stir until the noodles are evenly coated and hot.

Serve immediately, garnished with basil leaves and shredded spring onions.

For pork with red pepper, orange & honey, omit the lime leaves, lemon grass stalk, fish sauce and sugar. Stir-fry the pork as above with the spring onions, red pepper and chillies, then add the soy sauce, grated rind of 1 orange and 3 teaspoons each fresh orange juice and honey. Add the drained noodles and cook as above. Serve garnished with orange wedges.

lemon grass fish skewers

Serves **4**
Preparation time **10 minutes**
Cooking time **5 minutes**

500 g (1 lb) skinless and
    boneless **haddock fillets**,
    chopped
1 tablespoon chopped **mint**
2 tablespoons chopped **fresh
    coriander**
2 teaspoons **red Thai curry
    paste**
2 **lime leaves**, finely chopped,
    or the grated rind of 1 **lime**
2 **lemon grass stalks**,
    quartered lengthways
sunflower oil, for brushing

To serve
ready-made **sweet chilli
    sauce**
4 **lime wedges**

Put the haddock, mint, coriander, curry paste and
lime leaves or rind in a food processor or blender
and process for 30 seconds until well combined.

Shape the mixture into 8 portions and form each
around a lemon grass stalk 'skewer'.

Brush with a little oil and cook under a preheated hot
grill for 4—5 minutes or until cooked through. Serve
with a little sweet chilli sauce and lime wedges.

For rosemary swordfish skewers, replace the
haddock with 500 g (1 lb) boneless swordfish, use
8 rosemary stalks instead of the lemon grass and omit
the curry paste and coriander. Soak the rosemary
stalks in water. Blend the swordfish with the mint and
the grated rind of 1 lemon. Season well and shape
around the rosemary stalks. Cook as above and serve
with lemon wedges. You may need to protect any
exposed rosemary stalk with tin foil during grilling.

bean casserole with parsley pesto

Serves **4**
Preparation time **15 minutes**
Cooking time **20 minutes**

75 g (3 oz) **pancetta cubes**
1 **onion**, chopped
1 **garlic clove**, chopped
1 tablespoon chopped **thyme**
1 **carrot**, peeled and diced
400 g (13 oz) can **cannellini
   beans**, drained and rinsed
400 g (13 oz) can **chopped
   tomatoes**
200 ml (7 fl oz) **chicken stock**
1 tablespoon **tomato purée**
½ teaspoon **mustard powder**
salt and pepper
Parmesan cheese shavings,
   to serve

Parsley pesto
20 g (¾ oz) **flat leaf parsley**
1 **garlic clove**
25 g (1 oz) **pine nuts**, toasted
1 tablespoon **extra virgin
   olive oil**

Heat a large, nonstick frying pan and dry-fry the pancetta until it is soft. Add the onion, garlic, thyme and carrot, then stir in the beans, tomatoes, stock, tomato purée and mustard powder. Season to taste and simmer for 10 minutes or until the sauce has thickened.

Meanwhile, make the pesto. Mix together the parsley, garlic, pine nuts and oil and season to taste.

Serve the pancetta and bean mixture with the parsley pesto and Parmesan shavings.

For parsley pesto salad, simmer 200 g (7 oz) long-grain rice for 12 minutes or until tender, then drain, refresh with cold water and drain again. Mix with a 400 g (13 oz) can cannellini beans, drained and rinsed, 150 g (5 oz) halved cherry tomatoes, 1 deseeded and chopped red pepper and the pesto.

prawns with green leaves

Serves **4**
Preparation time **10 minutes**
Cooking time **5 minutes**

olive oil spray
20 large raw **king prawns**,
  with shells intact
1 **garlic clove**, chopped
125 g (4 oz) **plum tomatoes**,
  chopped
50 g (2 oz) **rocket**
50 g (2 oz) **spinach leaves**,
  tough stalks removed
50 g (2 oz) **watercress**, tough
  stalks removed
1 tablespoon **lemon juice**
salt and pepper

Heat a large saucepan, spray it with the oil, add the prawns and garlic and season to taste. Cover tightly and cook, shaking the pan from time to time, for about 3 minutes or until the prawns are cooked.

Add the tomatoes, rocket, spinach and watercress and stir until wilted. Squeeze over the lemon juice and check the seasoning.

Serve immediately, with French bread if liked.

For garlic mushrooms with green leaves, replace the prawns with 350 g (11½ oz) whole button mushrooms and cook with the garlic as above. Remove the mushrooms from the pan while you wilt the leaves and the tomatoes, then return them briefly to the pan. Serve topped with lemon rind and parsley.

chicken fajitas with tomato salsa

Serves **4**
Preparation time **15 minutes**,
   plus chilling
Cooking time **10 minutes**

1 tablespoon **olive oil**
1 large **red onion**, thinly sliced
1 **red pepper**, cored,
   deseeded and thinly sliced
1 **yellow pepper**, cored,
   deseeded and thinly sliced
450 g (14½ oz) skinless
   chicken breasts, cut into
   thin strips
⅛ teaspoon **paprika**
⅛ teaspoon **mild chilli powder**
⅛ teaspoon **cumin**
¼ teaspoon **oregano**
4 soft flour **tortillas**
½ **iceberg lettuce**, finely
   shredded

Tomato salsa
1 small **red onion**, finely
   chopped
425 g (14 oz) small **vine-
   ripened tomatoes**, chopped
2 **garlic cloves**, crushed
large handful of **fresh
   coriander leaves**, chopped
pepper

Make the salsa. Combine the onion, tomatoes, garlic and coriander in a bowl. Season with pepper, cover and chill for 30 minutes.

Heat the oil in a wok or large nonstick frying pan, add the onion and peppers and stir-fry for 3–4 minutes. Add the chicken, paprika, chilli powder, cumin and oregano and cook for a further 5 minutes or until the chicken is cooked through.

Meanwhile, wrap the tortillas in foil and warm them in the oven for 5 minutes or according to the instructions on the packet.

Spoon one-quarter of the chicken mixture into the centre of each tortilla, add a couple of tablespoons of salsa and some shredded lettuce. Roll up and serve warm.

For avocado salsa, peel, stone and finely dice 2 large ripe avocados and combine with 4 diced plum tomatoes, 1 finely chopped red onion, a 300 g (10 oz) can black-eyed beans, drained and rinsed, 2 tablespoons chopped fresh coriander and the grated rind and juice of 1 lime.

chinese chicken with peppers

Serves **4**
Preparation time **10 minutes**
Cooking time **18 minutes**

5 cm (2 inch) piece **fresh root
  ginger**, grated
2 **garlic cloves**, chopped
2 **star anise**
5 tablespoons ready-made
  teriyaki marinade
3 boneless, skinless **chicken
  breasts**, diced
sunflower oil spray
½ **red pepper**, cored,
  deseeded and diced
½ **green pepper**, cored,
  deseeded and diced
½ **yellow pepper**, cored,
  deseeded and diced
2 **spring onions**, sliced
300 g (10 oz) **easy-cook
  long-grain rice**
600 ml (1 pint) **chicken stock**

Mix together the ginger, garlic, star anise and teriyaki marinade. Add the chicken, turn to coat and set aside for 10 minutes.

Meanwhile, heat a frying pan, spray it lightly with oil and cook the peppers over medium heat for 3 minutes. Add the onion, rice and chicken and pour over the stock. Season to taste and simmer for 15 minutes, then serve hot.

For pork with green peppers and lychees, replace the chicken with 450 g (14½ oz) diced pork. Replace the peppers with 1½ diced green peppers and stir a 400 g (13 oz) can drained lychees into the pan with the onion, rice and pork.

minted courgette frittata

Serves **4**
Preparation time **10 minutes**
Cooking time **12–14 minutes**

4 teaspoons **olive oil**
1 **red onion**, thinly sliced
375 g (12 oz) **courgettes**,
   diced
6 **eggs**
2 tablespoons chopped **mint**
salt and pepper

Heat the oil in a large, nonstick frying pan with a flameproof handle, add the onion and courgettes and fry over gentle heat for 5 minutes or until lightly browned and just cooked.

Beat together the eggs, 2 tablespoons water, chopped mint and a little seasoning. Add the egg mixture to the frying pan. Cook, without stirring, for 4–5 minutes or until the frittata is almost set and the underside is golden brown.

Transfer the pan to a hot grill and cook for 3–4 minutes until the top is golden and the frittata is cooked through. Cut into wedges or squares and serve with a mixed salad, if liked.

For ham, black olive & courgette frittata, add 200 g (7 oz) diced, cooked ham and 50 g (2 oz) halved, pitted black olives to the pan with the onion and courgettes. Cook as above and serve with a cherry tomato and basil salad on shredded leaves.

chickpea & tomato casserole

Serves **4**
Preparation time **10 minutes**
Cooking time **about 30
minutes**

3 **garlic cloves**, crushed
3 **rosemary** sprigs
1 kg (2 lb) **vine tomatoes**,
halved
olive oil spray
1 mild **onion**, chopped
2 tablespoons **rosemary**
1 **red chilli**, deseeded and
chopped
50 ml (2 fl oz) **vegetable
stock**
2 x 410 g (13½ oz) cans
chickpeas, drained and
rinsed
salt and pepper

Stir the garlic and rosemary sprigs through the
tomatoes. Spread them out in a roasting tin and cook
in a preheated oven, 200°C (400°F), Gas Mark 6, for
30 minutes.

Meanwhile, lightly spray a casserole dish with oil and
gently cook the onion for 10 minutes. Add the chopped
rosemary, chilli, stock and chickpeas, season to taste,
cover and transfer to the oven for 20 minutes or the
remainder of the tomato cooking time.

When the tomatoes are cooked, stir them into the
chickpeas with all the juices from the roasting tin.
Check the seasoning and, if liked, serve with baked
potatoes and a green salad.

For sausage & tomato casserole, add 4 small, sliced
courgettes to the casserole dish with the onion. Grill
4 Toulouse sausages, then slice them and stir them
through the casserole when you add the tomatoes.
Serve with a leafy green salad.

grilled lamb with caperberries

Serves **4**
Preparation time **10 minutes**
Cooking time **10 minutes**

4 **lamb leg steaks**, about
   125 g (4 oz) each, fat
   trimmed off
6 tablespoons chopped **flat
   leaf parsley**, plus extra
   whole sprigs to garnish
1 **garlic clove**, crushed
12 **sun-dried tomatoes**
1 tablespoon **lemon juice**
1 tablespoon **olive oil**
2 tablespoons **caperberries**,
   rinsed
salt and pepper

Season the meat and cook under a preheated hot grill
for about 5 minutes on each side until golden.

Reserve 4 tablespoons of the chopped parsley. Blend
the remaining parsley with the garlic, tomatoes, lemon
juice and oil.

Spoon the tomato sauce over the lamb. Sprinkle over
the reserved chopped flat leaf parsley and add the
caperberries. Garnish with whole parsley sprigs and
serve with pasta, if liked.

For grilled lamb with tapenade, use black olive
tapenade instead of the dressing and stir all the
parsley through it. To make your own tapenade, whiz
150 g (5 oz) pitted black olives, 3 tablespoons extra
virgin olive oil, 1 garlic clove and 2 salted anchovies in
a food processor with black pepper and add chopped
flat leaf parsley to taste.

sesame tuna with spicy noodles

Serves **4**
Preparation time **10 minutes**
Cooking time **10 minutes**

300 g (10 oz) **rice vermicelli noodles**
50 g (2 oz) **sesame seeds**
4 **tuna steaks**, about 150 g (5 oz) each

Chilli dressing
2 **garlic cloves**, chopped
5 cm (2 inch) piece of **fresh root ginger**, peeled and grated
4 tablespoons **sweet chilli sauce**
20 g (¾ oz) **fresh coriander leaves**, plus extra to garnish
2 tablespoons **oil**
1 **chilli**, chopped
2 tablespoons **sesame oil**
2 tablespoons **rice vinegar**

Make the dressing by mixing together all the ingredients. Meanwhile, cook the noodles according to the instructions on the packet and set aside.

Press the sesame seeds into both sides of the tuna. Heat a large, heavy-based frying pan and dry-fry the tuna for 1–2 minutes on each side, depending on the thickness, until it is just pink in the middle.

Slice the tuna. Spoon the dressing over the hot noodles and put the sliced tuna on top. Garnish with coriander leaves and serve immediately.

For sesame tofu with shiitake mushrooms, substitute the tuna for 2 x 250 g (8 oz) blocks tofu, press in the sesame seeds and cook as above. Remove from the pan and slice. Fry 250 g (8 oz) fresh shiitake mushrooms in the pan after the tofu and mix in 2 chopped spring onions. Top the noodles with the mushrooms and sliced tofu and serve immediately.

quick prosciutto & rocket pizza

Serves **4**
Preparation time **10 minutes**
Cooking time **10 minutes**

4 mini **pizza bases**
2 **garlic cloves**, halved
250 g (8 oz) **reduced-fat mozzarella cheese**, shredded
8 **cherry tomatoes**, quartered
150 g (5 oz) **prosciutto**, sliced
50 g (2 oz) **rocket leaves**, washed
balsamic vinegar, to taste
salt and pepper

Rub the top surfaces of the pizza bases with the cut faces of the garlic cloves.

Put the pizza bases on a baking sheet, top with mozzarella and tomatoes and bake in a preheated oven, 200°C (400°F), Gas Mark 6, for 10 minutes until the bread is golden.

Top the pizzas with slices of prosciutto and rocket leaves, season to taste with salt, pepper and balsamic vinegar and serve immediately.

For tuna & pineapple pizza, drain and chop a 220 g (7½ oz) can pineapple, and drain and flake a 160 g (5½ oz) can tuna in spring water. Top the pizza bases with the pineapple and tuna then scatter over the mozzarella and tomatoes before cooking as above.

prawn, mango & avocado wrap

Serves **4**
Preparation time **10 minutes**,
  plus standing

2 tablespoons **low-fat crème
  fraîche**
2 teaspoons **tomato ketchup**
few drops of **Tabasco sauce**,
  to taste
300 g (10 oz) cooked peeled
  prawns
1 **mango**, peeled, stoned and
  thinly sliced
1 **avocado**, peeled, stoned
  and sliced
4 flour **tortillas**
100 g (3½ oz) **watercress**

Mix together the crème fraîche, ketchup and Tabasco to taste in a bowl.

Add the prawns, mango and avocado and toss the mixture together.

Spoon the mixture into the tortillas, add some sprigs of watercress, roll up and serve.

For tangy chicken wraps, marinate 300 g (10 oz) chicken in a mixture of 1 tablespoon fresh lemon or lime juice, I tablespoon Worcestershire sauce and 1 chopped garlic clove for 20 minutes. Cook the chicken under a preheated medium grill for 10 minutes, turning often. Slice and use instead of the prawns.

something
special

swordfish with couscous & salsa

Serves **4**
Preparation time **10 minutes**
Cooking time **10 minutes**

4 **swordfish steaks**, about
    150 g (5 oz) each
4–5 small ripe **tomatoes**
16 Kalamata **olives** in brine,
    drained
2 tablespoons chopped **flat
    leaf parsley**
salt and pepper
200 g (7 oz) **couscous**

Season the swordfish steaks with salt and pepper.

Dice or quarter the tomatoes and transfer them to a
bowl with all the juices. Remove the stones from the
olives and chop the flesh if the pieces are still large.
Stir them into the tomatoes with parsley, season to
taste and set aside.

Cook the couscous according to the instructions on
the packet and set aside.

Meanwhile, cook the swordfish steaks, 2 at a time, in
a preheated hot griddle pan. Cook on the first side for
4 minutes, without disturbing them, then turn and cook
for a further minute.

Serve the swordfish and couscous immediately, topped
with the olive and tomato salsa and accompanied with
a green salad, if liked.

For hake with pasta & salsa, replace the couscous
with 200 g (7 oz) tagliatelle or baby pasta shapes
and cook according to the packet instructions.
Replace the swordfish with 4 hake fillets and cook
as described above. When the pasta is cooked, toss
with the chopped parsley and a handful of chopped
capers. Serve the hake and pasta as above, topped
with the salsa.

japanese rice with nori

Serves **4**
Preparation time **10 minutes**
Cooking time **15 minutes**

225 g (7½ oz) **Japanese sushi** or **glutinous rice**
2 tablespoons black or white **sesame seeds**
1 teaspoon **coarse salt**
1 tablespoon **groundnut** or **vegetable oil**
2 **eggs**, beaten
4 **spring onions**, finely sliced
1 **red chilli**, deseeded and sliced
4 tablespoons **seasoned rice vinegar**
2 teaspoons **caster sugar**
1 tablespoon **light soy sauce**
25 g (1 oz) **pickled Japanese ginger**
2 sheets of **roasted nori** (seaweed)

Put the rice in a saucepan with 400 ml (14 fl oz) water. Bring to the boil, then reduce the heat and simmer, uncovered, for about 5 minutes until all the water is absorbed. Cover the pan and set aside for a further 5 minutes, until the rice is cooked.

Meanwhile, put the sesame seeds and salt in a frying pan and heat gently for about 2 minutes until the seeds are toasted. Remove and set aside.

Heat the oil in the pan, add the eggs and cook gently until just firm. Slide the omelette on to a plate, roll it up and cut it across into shreds.

Transfer the cooked rice to a bowl and stir in the spring onions, chilli, rice vinegar, sugar, soy sauce, ginger and half the toasted sesame seeds. Crumble 1 sheet of nori over the rice and stir in with the omelette shreds.

Transfer to a serving dish. Crumble the remaining nori over the rice, scatter with the remaining toasted sesame seeds and serve immediately.

For noodle & chicken salad, replace the rice with 200 g (7 oz) wheat and buckwheat noodles, cooked according to packet instructions. Omit the omelette and stir-fry 200 g (8 oz) shredded, cooked chicken in the oil instead.

bass with tomato & basil sauce

Serves **4**
Preparation time **10 minutes**
Cooking time **30 minutes**

8 **plum tomatoes**, halved
2 tablespoons **lemon juice**
grated rind of **1 lemon,** plus
   extra to garnish
4 **sea bass fillets**, about
   150 g (5 oz) each
2 tablespoons chopped **basil**
2 tablespoons extra virgin
   olive oil
salt and pepper

To garnish
basil leaves
lemon wedges

Make the sauce up to 2 days in advance. Arrange the tomatoes in a roasting tin, season well and cook in a preheated oven, 200°C (400°F), Gas Mark 6, for 20 minutes.

Transfer the tomatoes and any cooking juices to a pan and heat through gently with the lemon juice and rind. Season to taste and set aside until ready to serve.

Season the fish fillets and cook under a preheated hot grill for approximately 10 minutes or until the fish is cooked through.

Meanwhile, warm the sauce through. Stir the basil and oil through the sauce and spoon it over the fish. Garnish with basil leaves, more grated lemon rind and lemon wedges.

For tiger prawns in tomato & basil sauce, replace the bass fillets with 16 raw and peeled tiger prawns. Fry the prawns in a little oil spray until pink and cooked through. Make the sauce as above and spoon over the top of the cooked prawns to serve.

salmon & puy lentils with parsley

Serves **4**
Preparation time **15 minutes**
Cooking time **35 minutes**

200 g (7 oz) **Puy lentils**
1 **bay leaf**
200 g (7 oz) fine **green beans**, chopped
25 g (1 oz) **flat leaf parsley**, chopped
2 tablespoons **Dijon mustard**
2 tablespoons **capers**, rinsed and chopped
2 tablespoons **olive oil**
2 **lemons**, finely sliced
about 500 g (1 lb) **salmon fillets**
1 **fennel bulb**, finely sliced
salt and pepper
dill sprigs, to garnish

Put the lentils into a saucepan with the bay leaf and enough cold water to cover (do not add salt). Bring to the boil, reduce to a simmer and cook for 30 minutes or until tender. Season to taste, add the beans and simmer for 1 minute. Drain the lentils and stir in the parsley, mustard, capers and oil. Discard the bay leaf.

Meanwhile, arrange the lemon slices on a foil-lined grill pan and put the salmon and fennel slices on top. Season the salmon and fennel and cook under a preheated hot grill for about 10 minutes or until the salmon is cooked through.

Serve the fennel slices and lentils with the salmon on top, garnished with dill sprigs.

For pork escalopes with lentils, prepare the Puy lentils as above and replace the salmon with 4 pork escalopes. Grill the pork as above, omitting the fennel. Meanwhile, finely slice 2 celery sticks and toss with a little walnut oil. Serve the lentils with the escalopes on top, garnished with the celery and walnut oil.

monkfish with beans & pesto

Serves **4**
Preparation time **10 minutes**
Cooking time **10–15 minutes**

500 g (1 lb) **monkfish**, cut
   into 12 pieces
12 slices of **Parma ham**
12 **cherry tomatoes**
2 **yellow peppers**, cored,
   deseeded and cut
   into 6 wedges
2 tablespoon **olive oil**
300 g (10 oz) can **cannellini
   beans**, rinsed and drained
4 tablespoons **ready-made
   pesto**

Presoak 4 wooden skewers in warm water. Wrap each piece of monkfish in a slice of Parma ham. Thread these on to skewers, alternating with tomatoes and pieces of yellow pepper. Brush the kebabs with the oil and cook under a preheated hot grill for 3–4 minutes. Turn the skewers over and cook for a further 3 minutes until cooked through.

Put the beans in a nonstick saucepan and cook, stirring, over low heat for 4–5 minutes or until hot. Stir in the pesto.

Spoon the beans on to 4 plates, top with the kebabs and serve immediately.

For scallops with green beans & pesto, replace the monkfish with 16 scallops, wrap each one in a piece of Parma ham and skewer as above, omitting the peppers. Grill as above. Replace the cannellini beans with 250 g (8 oz) green beans and cook as above. Serve immediately, with crusty French bread.

lamb stuffed with rice & peppers

Serves **4**
Preparation time **40 minutes**
Cooking time **1 hour
20 minutes**

2 **red peppers**, cored,
    deseeded and halved
50 g (2 oz) **wild rice**, cooked
5 **garlic cloves**, chopped
5 **semi-dried tomatoes**,
    chopped
2 tablespoons chopped **flat
    leaf parsley**
625 g (1¼ lb) **boneless leg
    of lamb**, butterflied
salt and pepper
4 **artichoke halves**

Put the pepper halves in a roasting tin and cook in a
preheated oven, 180°C (350°F), Gas Mark 4, for
20 minutes, until the skin has blackened and blistered.
Cover with damp kitchen paper and set aside. When
the peppers are cool enough to handle, peel off the
skin and chop the flesh. (Leave the oven on.)

Mix together one of the chopped peppers, the rice,
garlic, tomatoes and parsley. Season to taste.

Put the lamb on a board and make a horizontal
incision, almost all the way along, to make a cavity for
stuffing. Fold back the top half, spoon in the stuffing
and fold back the top. Secure with skewers.

Cook the lamb for 1 hour, basting frequently and
adding the artichokes and other pepper for the last
15 minutes of cooking time. Slice the lamb and serve
immediately with roasted new potatoes, if liked.

For lamb stuffed with coriander & mint, combine
the grated rind and juice of 1 lime, 2 finely chopped
spring onions, 2 tablespoons each chopped fresh
coriander and chopped mint, 2 tablespoons olive oil,
2 finely chopped garlic cloves, and season. Spoon
over the lamb, roll and skewer, then roast as above.

sesame & ginger wraps

Serves **4**
Preparation time **15 minutes**
Cooking time **5–10 minutes**

Sesame and ginger sauce
1 **garlic clove**, chopped
5 cm (2 inch) piece **fresh root ginger**, peeled and roughly chopped
3 tablespoons **light muscovado sugar**
4 teaspoons **soy sauce**
5 teaspoons **wine** or **rice vinegar**
2 tablespoons **tomato purée**
2 tablespoons **sesame seeds**, plus extra to garnish

Pancakes
8 **rice pancakes**
2 **carrots**
100 g (3½ oz) **bean sprouts** or mixed **sprouting beans**
small handful of **mint**, roughly chopped
1 **celery stick**, thinly sliced
4 **spring onions**, thinly sliced diagonally
1 tablespoon **soy sauce**

Put all the ingredients for the sauce, except the sesame seeds, in a food processor or blender and process to a thin paste. Alternatively, crush the garlic, and grate the ginger and whisk into the remaining ingredients. Stir in the sesame seeds and transfer to a serving bowl.

Soften the rice pancakes according to the instructions on the packet. Cut the carrots into fine shreds and mix with the bean sprouts or sprouting beans, mint, celery, spring onions and soy sauce.

Spoon the vegetable mixture into the centre of each pancake. Fold in the bottom edge of each to the middle, then roll up from one side to the other to form a pocket.

Steam the pancakes for about 5 minutes until they are heated through. Alternatively, place them on a wire rack set over a roasting tin of boiling water and cover with foil. Serve immediately with the sauce and garnished with extra sesame seeds.

For veggie pancakes with plum & wasabi sauce, cook 250 g (8 oz) stoned and chopped ripe red plums in a saucepan, covered, with 2 tablespoons water until soft. Purée with 1 tablespoon soy sauce then add wasabi sauce and caster sugar to taste. Make the pancakes as above and serve drizzled with the plum and wasabi sauce.

lime & chilli marinated chicken

Serves **4**
Preparation time **15–20
minutes**, plus marinating
Cooking time **10 minutes**

4 boneless, skinless **chicken
breasts**, about 125 g (4 oz)
each
4 **limes**
2 **garlic cloves**, chopped
2 tablespoons chopped **dried**
or **fresh red chilli**
50 ml (2 fl oz) **sunflower oil**
200 g (7 oz) **rice noodles**
2 tablespoons chopped **fresh
coriander**, to garnish
salt and pepper

Presoak about 12 wooden skewers in warm water.
Cut the chicken into strips.

Grate the rind and squeeze the juice from 2 limes and
mix with the garlic, chilli and oil. Toss the chicken in the
lime and chilli mix, season with salt and pepper and set
aside for 1 hour.

Thread pieces of chicken on to skewers, not
overloading each one. Halve the remaining limes. Cook
the chicken and lime halves under a preheated hot grill
or on a preheated griddle for about 10 minutes.

Meanwhile, cook the noodles according to the
instructions on the packet.

Serve the chicken with the noodles, garnished with
coriander, and the caramelized lime halves.

For chicken tikka, finely chop 1 onion, 1 large
deseeded chilli, a 2 cm (¾ inch) piece fresh root
ginger and 2 finely chopped garlic cloves. Combine
with 150 g (5 oz) low-fat natural yogurt, 3 teaspoons
mild curry paste and 4 tablespoons chopped fresh
coriander. Marinate the chicken, then grill and serve
as above.

lamb fillet with vegetables

Serves **4**
Preparation time **20 minutes**
Cooking time **35–45 minutes**

500 g (1 lb) even-sized baby
  new potatoes
1 tablespoon chopped
  rosemary
400 g (13 oz) **lamb fillet**,
  diced
3 **garlic cloves**, halved
390 g (12½ oz) can
  artichokes, drained, rinsed
  and halved
1 **red pepper**, deseeded and
  quartered
200 g (7 oz) small **leeks**
salt and pepper

Put the potatoes in a pan with plenty of lightly salted water and bring to the boil. Drain immediately and toss with the rosemary.

Transfer the potatoes to a roasting tin with the lamb, garlic, artichokes and peppers. Cover and cook in a preheated oven, 180°C (350°F), Gas Mark 4, for 30–40 minutes or until cooked through and the potato skins are golden. Meanwhile, steam the leeks.

Drain the excess fat and serve the lamb with the roasted vegetables, leeks and any pan juices.

For herby baked lamb, before baking sprinkle the diced lamb with 6–8 tablespoons lemon juice, ¼ teaspoon each dried oregano and thyme, the leaves torn from 2 oregano sprigs, 4 lemon thyme sprigs and salt and pepper.

pork fillet with soy-garlic marinade

Serves **4**

Preparation time **5 minutes**, plus marinating

Cooking time **20 minutes**

2 **pork fillets**, 250 g (8 oz) each

1 tablespoon **linseeds**

150 ml (¼ pint) **dry white wine**

Soy and garlic marinade

1 **cinnamon stick**

2 tablespoons **soy sauce**

2 **garlic cloves**, crushed

1 teaspoon grated **fresh root ginger**

1 tablespoon **clear honey**

1 teaspoon crushed **coriander seeds**

1 teaspoon **sesame oil**

Mix together the ingredients for the marinade. Put the pork in a shallow, non-metallic dish, cover evenly with the marinade and leave for at least 2–3 hours, preferably overnight.

Drain the pork, reserving the marinade. Press the linseeds into the pork so that both sides of each fillet are evenly covered.

Heat an ovenproof frying pan over a high heat on the hob. Seal the pork and transfer it to a preheated oven, 180°C (350°F), Gas Mark 4. Cook for 18–20 minutes or until golden brown.

Meanwhile, remove the cinnamon stick from the marinade and pour the liquid into a nonstick pan. Add the wine and bring to the boil. Reduce the heat and simmer until it has the consistency of a sticky glaze. Remove from the heat and set aside.

Remove the pork from the oven and cut it into 5 mm (¼ inch) slices. Serve on a bed of steamed vegetables, such as pak choi or spinach, and drizzle the glaze over the pork.

For pork with orange marinade, mix the grated rind of 1 orange with 3 crushed garlic cloves, the crushed seeds from 8 cardamom pods and a little salt and pepper. Marinate and cook the pork as above.

prawns with lemon & tomato

Serves **4**
Preparation time **10 minutes**
Cooking time **30–40 minutes**

olive oil spray
1 **onion**, chopped
2 **garlic cloves**, finely
  chopped
1 **carrot**, finely chopped
1 **celery stick**, finely chopped
25 ml (1 fl oz) **white wine**
400 g (13 oz) can **chopped
  tomatoes**
300 g (10 oz) raw **tiger
  prawns**, shells removed
grated rind of 1 **lemon**
750 g (1½ lb) **new potatoes**,
  cut into even sizes
1 tablespoon **olive oil**
50 g (2 oz) **rocket**,
  to garnish
salt and pepper

Lightly spray a medium saucepan with oil, add the onion, garlic, carrot and celery and cook gently for about 15 minutes or until soft. (Add a few drops of water if the pan gets too dry.) Increase the heat and stir in the wine. Add the tomatoes, reduce to a simmer and cook for 10 minutes until the sauce is smooth and thick.

Add the prawns and simmer for 3–4 minutes or until the prawns are just cooked. Stir in half the lemon rind.

Meanwhile, steam the potatoes, then toss them in the remaining lemon rind, pepper and oil. Serve them with the prawns, garnished with rocket.

For smoked haddock & eggs with lemon & tomato, poach 400 g (13 oz) smoked haddock instead of the prawns. Cook the tomato sauce as above and stir through 4 hard-boiled and quartered eggs with the haddock. Serve with cooked pasta and garnish with a handful of parsley.

chicken with pesto & polenta

Serves **4**
Preparation time **15 minutes**
Cooking time **10 minutes**

4 **chicken breasts**, about
   125 g (4 oz) each
25 g (1 oz) **basil leaves**
2 tablespoons **olive oil**
2 tablespoons **pine nuts**,
   toasted
1 **garlic clove**, peeled
2 tablespoons grated
   Parmesan cheese
25 g (1 oz) **rocket leaves**
200 g (7 oz) instant **polenta**
salt and pepper

Slice the chicken breasts horizontally through the middle and season all 8 pieces.

Put the basil, oil, pine nuts, garlic, Parmesan and rocket together in a food processor or blender and process until finely chopped. Set aside.

Cook the chicken under a preheated hot grill for 5–7 minutes until just cooked through and still succulent.

Meanwhile, stir the polenta into 800 ml (18 fl oz) lightly salted boiling water and keep stirring for about 2 minutes while it cooks. Stir the rocket pesto through the polenta.

Serve the chicken slices on top of the polenta.

For chicken with mixed vegetable mash, replace the polenta with 500 g (1 lb) potatoes and 250 g (8 oz) each swede and carrots. Boil the vegetables for 12–15 minutes until soft then mash to a creamy consistency. Swirl the rocket pesto through the mash.

yellow split pea & pepper patties

Serves **4**
Preparation time **10–15
 minutes**, plus chilling
Cooking time **40–50 minutes**

3 **garlic cloves**
250 g (8 oz) **yellow split
 peas**
750 ml (1¼ pints) **vegetable
 stock**
olive oil spray
2 **red peppers**, halved and
 deseeded
1 **yellow pepper**, halved and
 deseeded
1 **red onion**, quartered
1 tablespoon chopped **mint**
2 tablespoons **capers**, rinsed
 and chopped
flour, for dusting
salt and pepper
ready-made **tzatziki** or **raita**,
 to serve

Peel and halve a garlic clove and cook it with the split peas in the stock for 40 minutes. Check the seasoning and leave to cool slightly.

Meanwhile, lightly spray a roasting tin with oil. Put the remaining garlic cloves in the tin with the peppers and onion and cook in a preheated oven, 200°C (400°F), Gas Mark 6, for 20 minutes. Squeeze the roasted garlic cloves from their skins and chop with the roasted vegetables.

Mix the split peas with the roasted vegetables, mint and capers. Flour your hands and shape the mixture into patties. Refrigerate until ready to cook.

Heat a frying pan and spray with oil. Cook the patties, in batches if necessary, leaving them to cook undisturbed for 2 minutes on each side. Serve either hot or cold, garnished with mint leaves, with tzatziki or raita on the side.

For homemade tzatziki, finely chop ½ cucumber and combine with 1 pressed garlic clove, 2 tablespoons chopped fresh mint and 300 ml (½ pint) yogurt.

chicken with paprika & red wine

Serves **4**
Preparation time **15 minutes**
Cooking time **30–40 minutes**

1 **garlic bulb**
625 g (1¼ lb) **new potatoes**
1 tablespoon chopped
  rosemary
2 tablespoons **olive oil**
4 boneless, skinless **chicken
  breasts**, about 150 g (5 oz)
  each, diced
1 mild **Spanish onion,**
  chopped
1 **red pepper**, cored,
  deseeded and chopped
1 **bay leaf**
3 **thyme** sprigs
1 tablespoon **smoked
  paprika** (pimentón)
400 ml (14 fl oz) **red wine**
250 ml (8 fl oz) **chicken stock**
salt and pepper

Roast the whole garlic bulb in a preheated oven, 200°C (400°F), Gas Mark 6, for 30 minutes. At the same time, roast the potatoes for 30 minutes with a little rosemary and salt.

Heat the oil in a saucepan and cook the chicken until golden. Add the onion, red pepper, bay leaf, thyme and smoked paprika, season to taste and cook, stirring frequently, until the vegetables are soft. Add the wine and stock and cook for 20 minutes to reduce.

Squeeze the soft pulp from the cooked garlic and add it to the chicken to taste. Season with more pepper if necessary.

Remove the bay leaf and thyme and serve the chicken with the roast potatoes and, if liked, baby courgettes and carrots or shredded green cabbage.

For pancetta & mushroom in red wine, replace the chicken with 200 g (7 oz) diced pancetta or streaky bacon. Continue as above, omitting the roasted garlic. Simmer and add 200 g (7 oz) halved mushrooms 5 minutes before the end of cooking. Serve as above.

beef fillet with red pepper crust

Serves **4**
Preparation time **15 minutes**
Cooking time **about 30 minutes**

1 **red pepper,** halved and deseeded
2 **garlic cloves**
8 dry **black olives,** pitted
2 teaspoons **olive oil**
2 teaspoons **capers**
8 **shallots,** peeled
50 ml (2 fl oz) **balsamic vinegar**
1 teaspoon **light muscovado sugar**
4 **beef fillet steaks,** about 100 g (3½ oz) each
salt and pepper

Cook the pepper under a preheated hot grill until the skin blackens. Remove and cover with damp kitchen paper until it is cool enough to handle, then peel and chop.

Blend together the garlic, olives, 1 teaspoon oil, the capers and the chopped red pepper.

Put the shallots and the remaining oil in a small pan. Cover and cook, stirring frequently, over low heat for 15 minutes. Add the vinegar and sugar and cook uncovered, stirring frequently, for a further 5 minutes.

Season the steaks and cook, 2 at a time, in a preheated heavy-based frying pan or griddle pan. Cook on one side, then transfer to a baking sheet. Top each steak with some red pepper mix. Bake in a preheated oven, 200°C (400°F), Gas Mark 6, for 5 minutes or according to taste. Leave to stand in a warm place for 5 minutes before serving with the balsamic shallots and, if liked, steamed wholegrain rice.

For beef fillet with mushroom crust, blend 350 g (11½ oz) chopped mushrooms with 2 crushed garlic cloves, 1 chopped onion, 2 teaspoons olive oil and seasoning. Cook as above for 10 minutes or until reduced down to concentrate. Add juice of ½ lemon, 2 tablespoons chopped fresh parsley and a dash of brandy, then cook for a further 5 minutes. Cook the steaks as above and top with the mushroom mixture.

pork fillet with fennel & pepper

Serves **4**
Preparation time **20 minutes**
Cooking time **1 hour**

2 **garlic cloves**, sliced
2 teaspoon **light muscovado sugar**
2 tablespoons **balsamic vinegar**
500 g (1 lb) **pork fillet**
1 **red pepper**, cored, deseeded and cut into 8 wedges
2 **fennel bulbs**, finely sliced
50 ml (2 fl oz) **chicken stock**
1 tablespoon **olive oil**
200 g (7 oz) **broccoli**, sliced
8 **semi-dried tomato quarters**
salt and pepper

Mix together the garlic, sugar and vinegar, and season to taste. Put the pork in a non-metallic dish, pour over the marinade and set aside while you prepare the vegetables.

Put together in a roasting tin the red pepper, fennel, stock and oil. Add salt and pepper and cook in a preheated oven, 200°C (400°F), Gas Mark 6, for 40 minutes.

Drain the pork (discard the marinade), add it to the vegetables in the roasting tin and cook for 20 minutes or until it is just cooked and golden and the juices run clear. Add the broccoli and tomatoes for the last 10 minutes of cooking time.

Slice the pork, arrange the fennel, broccoli and red pepper over the slices and spoon over any pan juices. Serve with basmati and wild rice, if liked.

For creamy sweet potato mash, to serve as an accompaniment, boil 1 kg (2 lb) sweet potatoes for 12 minutes or until soft. Mash with 100 g (3½ oz) low-fat soft cheese and add a handful of chopped chives and a pinch of cinnamon.

indonesian prawn salad

Serves **4**
Preparation time **20 minutes**
Cooking time **5 minutes**

125 g (4 oz) **rice noodles**
65 g (2½ oz) **cucumber**, thinly sliced
2 tablespoons **rice vinegar**
2 tablespoons **caster sugar**
1 **egg**, beaten
oil spray
4 **shallots**, sliced
2 **garlic cloves**, crushed
1 teaspoon grated **fresh root ginger**
1 teaspoon **ground coriander**
2 **peppers**, chopped
3 **red chillies**, sliced
1 tablespoon **Thai fish sauce**
250 g (8 oz) cooked peeled **prawns**
1 tablespoon **soy sauce**
salt

To serve
fresh coriander leaves
3 tablespoons chopped roasted **peanuts**
2 spring onions, finely sliced
prawn crackers

Cook the noodles according to the instructions on the packet. Drain, rinse well and set aside.

Pickle the cucumber in equal quantities of rice vinegar and sugar for 5 minutes, drain and set aside.

Mix the egg with 3 tablespoons water. Spray a wok or large frying pan with oil and, when it is quite hot, make a thin omelette with the egg mixture. Roll it up, leave to cool and cut into thin strips.

Combine the shallots, garlic, ginger and ground coriander in a large bowl. Add the peppers, chillies, fish sauce, prawns and noodles and mix in, using 2 spoons to lift and stir, until they are thoroughly combined. Add the soy sauce and salt to taste.

Transfer to a serving dish and serve with the omelette strips, pickled cucumber, coriander leaves, peanuts and spring onions, and with prawn crackers on the side.

For hot & sweet pork with rice, cook 250 g (8 oz) rice according to the packet instructions, instead of the noodles. Meanwhile, stir-fry 250 g (8 oz) lean boneless pork strips until cooked, then mix with the hot rice and dressed prawns. Garnish with the omelette and pickled cucumber, as above.

tamarind & lemon grass beef

Serves **4**
Preparation time **15 minutes**
Cooking time **12 minutes**

1 tablespoon **oil**
500 g (1 lb) lean **beef**, cut
  into strips
2 **lemon grass stalks**,
  chopped
6 **shallots,** chopped
2 **green chillies**, chopped
3 tablespoons **tamarind
  paste**
2 tablespoons **lime juice**
2 teaspoons **Thai fish sauce**
2 teaspoons **brown sugar**
200 g (7 oz) shredded **green
  papaya**

Heat the oil in a wok or frying pan, toss in the meat
and cook over a high heat for 2—3 minutes.

Add the lemon grass, shallots and chillies and stir-fry
for a further 5 minutes or until the meat is well browned.

Add the tamarind paste, lime juice, fish sauce, sugar
and papaya and stir-fry for a further 4 minutes.

Serve immediately, if liked with coconut rice and
a salad.

For tofu with tamarind & lemon grass, proceed
as above but replace the beef with 250 g (8 oz)
tofu, drained and sliced. Stir-fry 125 g (4 oz) each
mangetout and sliced shiitake mushrooms in place of
the papaya and replace the fish sauce with soy sauce.

vegetarian

chickpea & tomato soup

Serves **4**
Preparation time **15 minutes**
Cooking time **10 minutes**

1 tablespoon **olive oil**
1 **onion**, roughly chopped
1 **garlic clove**, crushed
1 **carrot**, roughly chopped
1 **red pepper**, cored,
   deseeded and roughly
   chopped
1 teaspoon **cumin seeds**
500 ml (17 fl oz) hot
   vegetable stock
400 g (13 oz) can **chopped
   tomatoes**
410 g (13½ oz) can
   chickpeas, drained and
   rinsed
20 g (¾ oz) each **pumpkin,
   sesame and sunflower
   seeds**
2 tablespoons chopped **fresh
   coriander**
salt and pepper

Heat the oil in a large saucepan over medium heat, add the onion, garlic, carrot, red pepper and cumin seeds and stir-fry for about 1 minute. Add the stock and tomatoes and simmer for 5 minutes until the vegetables are soft.

Meanwhile, dry-fry the garnish seeds in a pan over medium heat until they are golden. Set aside to cool.

Remove the vegetable pan from the heat and use a hand-held blender to purée the vegetables. Alternatively, mash them by hand. Stir through the chickpeas and heat through for 2 minutes.

Season to taste, sprinkle over the roasted seeds and fresh coriander and serve with crusty mixed grain bread, if liked.

For tomato & pepper casserole, halve the amount of stock and cook the vegetables as above, but do not blend. Prepare 250 g (8 oz) couscous by pouring over boiling water to a depth of 2.5 cm (1 inch). Leave to stand for a few minutes before separating the grains with a fork and serving with the casserole.

carrot & chickpea soup

Serves **4**
Preparation time **25 minutes**
Cooking time **about 40 minutes**

1 tablespoon **sunflower oil**
1 large **onion**, chopped
500 g (1 lb) **carrots**, diced
1 teaspoon **ground cumin**
1 teaspoon **fennel seeds**, roughly crushed
2 cm (¾ inch) **fresh root ginger**, peeled and finely chopped
1 **garlic clove**, finely chopped
410 g (13½ oz) can **chickpeas**, drained
1.2 litres (2 pints) **vegetable stock**
300 ml (½ pint) **semi-skimmed milk**
salt and pepper

To garnish
1 teaspoon **sunflower oil**
40 g (1½ oz) **flaked almonds**
pinch of ground **cumin**
pinch of **paprika**

Heat the oil in a saucepan, add the onion and fry gently, stirring, for 5 minutes or until lightly browned. Mix in the carrots, ground spices, ginger and garlic and cook for 1 minute.

Mix in the chickpeas, stock and a little seasoning, bring to the boil, cover and simmer for 30 minutes or until the vegetables are tender.

Purée the soup in batches until smooth, in a food processor or blender, then return to the pan and stir in the milk. Reheat gently.

Meanwhile, make the garnish. Heat the oil in a small frying pan, add the almonds, cumin and paprika and cook for 2–3 minutes until golden brown.

Ladle the soup into bowls and top with the almonds, cumin and paprika. Serve with warm bread, if liked.

For carrot & lentil soup, substitute the chickpeas for a 410 g (13½ oz) can green lentils. You can also use cannellini beans or other canned pulses. Omit the milk, but add an extra 300 ml (½ pint) stock. Otherwise, proceed as above. Serve the soup, then swirl 1 teaspoon Greek yogurt through each bowl.

gazpacho

Serves **4**

Preparation time **15 minutes**, plus chilling

Cooking time **25 minutes**

750 g (1½ lb) ripe **tomatoes**
1 large **fennel bulb**
¾ teaspoon **coriander seeds**
½ teaspoon **mixed peppercorns**
1 tablespoon **extra virgin olive oil**
1 large **garlic clove**, crushed
1 small **onion**, chopped
1 tablespoon **balsamic vinegar**
1 tablespoon **lemon juice**
1 tablespoon chopped **oregano**
1 teaspoon **tomato purée**
1 rounded teaspoon **rock salt**
green olives, finely sliced, to garnish

Put the tomatoes in a large pan or bowl and pour over enough boiling water to cover. Leave for about 1 minute, then drain, skin carefully and roughly chop the flesh.

Trim the green fronds from the fennel and discard. Finely slice the bulb and put it in a saucepan with 300 ml (½ pint) lightly salted boiling water. Cover and simmer for 10 minutes.

Meanwhile, crush the coriander seeds and peppercorns using a pestle and mortar. Gently heat the oil in a large pan and add the crushed spices, garlic and onion. Cook gently for 5 minutes.

Add the vinegar, lemon juice, tomatoes and oregano, reserving a few oregano leaves to garnish. Give the mixture a good stir and add the fennel along with the cooking liquid, tomato purée and salt. Bring to a simmer and leave to cook, uncovered, for 10 minutes.

Transfer the soup to a food processor or blender and process lightly. Cool and chill overnight and serve garnished with the reserved oregano leaves and green olives.

For easy almond gazpacho, blend together in a food processor 250 g (8 oz) ground almonds, 750 ml (1¼ pints) iced water, 75 g (3 oz) breadcrumbs, 2 crushed garlic cloves, 3 tablespoons olive oil, a splash of white wine vinegar and seasoning. Chill for one hour and check seasoning again before serving.

roasted pepper & tomato soup

Serves **4**
Preparation time **10 minutes**
Cooking time **40 minutes**

4 **red peppers**, cored and
  deseeded
500 g (1 lb) **tomatoes**, halved
1 teaspoon **olive oil**
1 **onion**, chopped
1 **carrot**, chopped
600 ml (1 pint) **vegetable
  stock**
2 tablespoons **low-fat crème
  fraîche**
handful of **basil leaves**, torn
pepper

Put the peppers, skin side up, and the tomatoes, skin side down, on a baking sheet under a hot grill and cook for 8–10 minutes until the skins of the peppers are blackened. Cover the peppers with damp kitchen paper, leave to cool, then remove the skins and slice the flesh. Leave the tomatoes to cool, then remove the skins.

Heat the oil in a large saucepan, add the onion and carrot and fry for 5 minutes. Add the stock and the skinned roasted peppers and tomatoes, bring to the boil and simmer for 20 minutes until the carrot is tender.

Transfer the soup to a food processor or blender and process until smooth, in batches if necessary. Return to the pan and heat through gently. Stir through the crème fraîche and basil, season well with pepper and serve.

For roasted courgette & pea soup, replace the red peppers with 4 medium courgettes, sliced lengthways and roasted as above. Add 200 g (7 oz) frozen peas with the stock and bring to the boil. Check for seasoning and garnish with torn basil and mint.

chickpea & parsley soup

Serves **6**
Preparation time **15 minutes**,
   plus soaking
Cooking time **30 minutes**

1 small **onion**
3 **garlic cloves**
30 g (1½ oz) **parsley**
2 tablespoons **olive oil**
410 g (13½ oz) can
   chickpeas, drained and
   rinsed
1.2 litres (2 pints) **vegetable
   stock**
grated rind and juice of
   ½ **lemon**
salt and pepper

Put the onion, garlic and parsley in a food processor or blender and process until finely chopped.

Heat the oil in a saucepan and cook the onion mixture over a low heat until slightly softened. Add the chickpeas and cook gently for 1–2 minutes.

Add the stock, season well with salt and pepper and bring to the boil. Cover and cook for 20 minutes or until the chickpeas are really tender.

Allow the soup to cool for a while, then partly purée it in a food processor or blender or mash it with a fork so that it retains plenty of texture.

Pour the soup into a clean pan, add the lemon juice and adjust the seasoning if necessary. Heat through gently. Serve the soup topped with grated lemon rind and cracked black pepper.

For flageolet, cannellini & parsley soup, replace the chickpeas with 200 g (7 oz) each canned flageolet and cannellini beans, and use the rind and juice of 1 lemon. Otherwise, cook as above.

pea & lettuce soup with croûtons

Serves **4**
Preparation time **10 minutes**
Cooking time **25–30 minutes**

25 g (1 oz) **butter**
1 large **onion**, finely chopped
425 g (14 oz) frozen **peas**
2 **Little Gem lettuces**, roughly
  chopped
1 litre (1¾ pints) **vegetable
  stock**
grated rind and juice of
  ½ **lemon**
salt and pepper

Sesame croûtons
2 thick slices of **bread,** cubed
1 tablespoon **olive oil**
1 tablespoon **sesame seeds**

Make the croûtons. Brush the bread cubes with the oil and put them in a roasting tin. Sprinkle with the sesame seeds and cook in a preheated oven, 200°C (400°F), Gas Mark 6, for 10 minutes or until golden.

Meanwhile, heat the butter in a large saucepan, add the onion and cook for 5 minutes or until beginning to soften. Add the peas, lettuces, stock, lemon rind and juice and seasoning. Bring to the boil, reduce the heat, cover and simmer for 10 minutes.

Allow the soup to cool slightly, then transfer to a food processor or blender and process until smooth. Return the soup to the pan, adjust the seasoning if necessary and heat through gently.

Spoon the soup into warm serving bowls and serve sprinkled with the croûtons.

For minted pea & watercress soup, replace the lettuce with 100 g (3½ oz) watercress, torn into pieces. Cook the watercress as for lettuce, simmering for 10 minutes but omitting the lemon rind and juice. When returning the soup to the pan after processing, add 2 tablespoons chopped mint leaves.

spicy goan aubergine curry

Serves **4**
Preparation time **15 minutes**
Cooking time **20 minutes**

1 teaspoon **cayenne pepper**
2 fresh **green chillies**,
   deseeded and sliced
½ teaspoon **turmeric**
4 **garlic cloves**, crushed
2½ cm (1 inch) piece of **fresh
   root ginger**, peeled and
   grated
1 teaspoon **cumin seeds**,
   toasted
4 teaspoons **coriander seeds**,
   toasted
400 g (13 oz) can
   coconut milk
1 tablespoon **tamarind paste**
1 large **aubergine**, thinly
   sliced lengthways
salt and pepper

Mix together the cayenne, chillies, turmeric, garlic and ginger with 300 ml (½ pint) warm water.

Crush the cumin and coriander seeds together, add them to the sauce and simmer for 10 minutes until thickened. Season to taste. Stir in the coconut milk and tamarind paste.

Arrange the aubergine slices in a foil-lined grill pan and brush the tops with some of the curry sauce. Cook under a preheated hot grill until golden.

Serve the aubergine slices in the curry sauce and, if liked, with naan bread or chapattis.

For cashew nut curry, add 200 g (7 oz) roasted cashew nuts to the curry sauce. To roast, soak in water for 20 minutes, chop, then heat in a dry pan shaking regularly until lightly browned. Replace the aubergine with 4 sliced courgettes and grill as above. Drizzle with walnut oil and season well.

red rice & pumpkin risotto

Serves **4**
Preparation time **20 minutes**
Cooking time **35 minutes**

1 litre (1¾ pints) **vegetable stock**
250 g (8 oz) **Camargue red rice**
1 tablespoon **olive oil**
1 **onion**, finely chopped
2 **garlic cloves**, finely chopped
750 g (1½ lb) **pumpkin**, peeled, deseeded and diced
5 tablespoons finely chopped **fresh basil** or **oregano**, plus extra leaves to garnish
50 g (2 oz) **Parmesan cheese**, coarsely grated, plus shavings to garnish
salt and pepper

Put the stock in a large saucepan, add the rice and simmer for 35 minutes.

Meanwhile, heat the oil in a frying pan, add the onion and cook, stirring occasionally, for 5 minutes or until softened. Add the garlic, pumpkin and a little salt and pepper, mix together, then cover and cook over moderate heat for 10 minutes, stirring occasionally.

Drain the rice and reserve the cooking liquid. Stir the chopped herbs into the frying pan with the drained rice and grated Parmesan. Adjust the seasoning and moisten with the reserved rice liquid if necessary.

Spoon into shallow dishes and serve garnished with extra herbs and Parmesan shavings.

For crunchy cabbage salad, to serve as an accompaniment, blanch 250 g (8 oz) crisp green beans. Finely shred ¼ red cabbage and a handful fresh chopped parsley. Mix the beans, cabbage and parsley, then drizzle with walnut oil.

roasted pumpkin with feta

Serves **4**

Preparation time **10 minutes**

Cooking time **40 minutes**

625 g (1¼ lb) **pumpkin** or
  butternut squash, cut into
  5 cm (2 inch) wedges

2 tablespoons **olive oil**

1 tablespoon **lemon juice**

2 tablespoons chopped **mint**,
  plus shredded **mint** to
  garnish

200 g (7 oz) **feta cheese**

50 g (2 oz) **walnuts**, chopped

8 **sun-dried tomatoes**,
  chopped

85 g (3¼ oz) **baby spinach
  leaves**

salt and pepper

Toss the pumpkin pieces in 1 tablespoon oil, season
and spread out in a roasting tin. Roast in a preheated
oven, 200°C (400°F), Gas Mark 6, for 30 minutes.

Mix the remaining oil with the lemon juice and mint.
Spoon the mixture over the feta cheese and set aside.

Add the walnuts and the tomatoes to the pumpkin and
bake for a further 10 minutes.

Serve the pumpkin with the walnuts and tomatoes and
any pan juices. Crumble over the cheese and pour over
the marinade. Serve with the spinach leaves and
garnished with shredded mint.

**For roasted pumpkin with Stilton, walnuts & black
olives**, replace the tomatoes with 16 roughly chopped
black olives. Replace the feta with the same quantity
of Stilton and serve the salad with rocket leaves.

vegetable gratin with herby crust

Serves **4**
Preparation time **20 minutes**
Cooking time **45 minutes**

50 g (2 oz) **reduced-fat**
   sunflower spread
400 g (13 oz) waxy **potatoes**,
   peeled and sliced
200 g (7 oz) **sweet potato**,
   peeled and sliced
200 g (7 oz) **carrots**, sliced
2 **garlic cloves**, chopped
300 g (10 oz) **half-fat crème**
   fraîche
250 ml (8 fl oz) **vegetable**
   stock
1 tablespoon grated
   Parmesan cheese
2 tablespoons chopped **sage**
1 tablespoon chopped
   rosemary
75 g (3 oz) **breadcrumbs**
salt and pepper

Lightly grease a square ovenproof dish with the sunflower spread. Layer the sliced vegetables in the dish, adding a little garlic and seasoning between each layer.

Heat the crème fraîche with the stock and pour it over the vegetables.

Mix together the Parmesan, sage, rosemary and breadcrumbs, season and sprinkle over the vegetables. Bake in a preheated oven, 200°C (400°F), Gas Mark 6, for 45 minutes until golden and cooked through. Serve immediately.

For beetroot gratin with nutty crust, replace the carrot with 250 g (8 oz) sliced beetroot and cook as above. When preparing the topping, add 100 g (3½ oz) chopped pecans. Serve with a shredded red cabbage salad.

dhal patties with yogurt relish

Serves **4**

Preparation time **30 minutes**, plus chilling

Cooking time **20 minutes**

2 x 410 g (13½ oz) cans **green lentils**, drained and rinsed

500 ml (17 fl oz) **vegetable stock**

1 **bay leaf**

5 cm (2 inch) **cinnamon stick**

2 **cardamom pods**

2 tablespoons chopped **fresh coriander**

2 tablespoons chopped **mint**

1 **red onion**, finely sliced

250 g (8 oz) **fat-free yogurt**

250 g (8 oz) frozen **peas**

4 tablespoons **dhansak curry paste**, or to taste

sunflower oil spray

salt and pepper

Presoak some 15 cm (6 inch) wooden skewers in warm water. Combine the lentils with the stock, bay leaf, cinnamon stick and cardamom pods in a pan, season with salt and simmer for 10 minutes or until the lentils are soft.

Meanwhile, to make the yogurt relish, mix together the coriander, mint, onion and yogurt and add salt and pepper to taste.

Cook the peas in boiling water. Drain the lentils and remove the bay leaf, cinnamon stick and cardamom pods. Transfer the peas and lentils to a food processor or blender and process briefly. Stir the pea mixture into the curry paste and use 2 teaspoons to shape the mixture into small balls. Refrigerate until ready to cook.

Put 3–4 balls on each skewer. Heat a frying pan and spray it with oil. Fry the skewers (in batches if necessary) over medium heat for 2 minutes undisturbed, then turn and cook the other side. Serve hot with the yogurt relish.

For cucumber raita, slice, salt and drain 1 cucumber to remove the excess water, then combine it with ½ teaspoon each ground cumin and salt, 1 teaspoon each sugar and lemon juice and the fat-free yogurt.

stilton & leek tartlets

Serves **4**
Preparation time **15 minutes**
Cooking time **25 minutes**

1 teaspoon **olive oil**
8 small **leeks**, finely sliced
50 g (2 oz) **Stilton cheese**, crumbled
1 teaspoon chopped **thyme**
2 **eggs**, beaten
4 tablespoons **low-fat crème fraîche**
12 x 15 cm (6 inch) squares **filo pastry**
milk, for brushing

Heat the oil in a saucepan, add the leeks and fry for 3–4 minutes until softened.

Stir half the Stilton and the thyme into the leek mixture, then blend together the remaining Stilton, the eggs and crème fraîche in a bowl.

Brush the filo squares with a little milk and use them to line 4 fluted flan tins, each 10 cm (4 inches) across. Spoon the leek mixture into the tins, then pour over the cheese and egg mixture.

Place the tins on a baking sheet and bake in a preheated oven, 200°C (400°F), Gas Mark 6, for 15–20 minutes until the filling is set.

For spring onion & Cheddar tartlets, use the same quantity of mature Cheddar cheese instead of Stilton and grate it coarsely. Slice 2 bunches of large spring onions and fry for 1 minute, then remove from the heat. Add the spring onions and continue as above.

pilaf with nuts, lemon & herbs

Serves **4**
Preparation time **15 minutes**
Cooking time **10 minutes**

2 tablespoons **olive oil**
1 **mild onion**, chopped
2 **garlic cloves**, crushed
300 ml (½ pint) **vegetable stock**
500 g (1 lb) **couscous**
1 **pomegranate**
50 g (2 oz) **pine nuts**, toasted
3 tablespoons chopped **flat leaf parsley**
3 tablespoons chopped **dill**
3 tablespoons chopped **fresh coriander**
grated rind and juice of 1 **lemon**
salt and pepper

Heat the oil in a large frying pan and cook the onion and garlic for about 5 minutes or until soft. Add the stock and heat, then add the couscous. Stir, cover and leave to steam over gentle heat for 5 minutes.

Meanwhile, take the seeds from the pomegranate, working over a bowl to catch any juice.

When the couscous is cooked, stir in the nuts and herbs and a little salt and pepper.

Mix together the pomegranate seeds and juice and lemon rind and juice. Spoon over the couscous just before serving.

For grilled marinated haloumi, to serve as an accompaniment, slice 250 g (8 oz) haloumi into 8 pieces and marinate in the juice of 1 lemon, a dash of olive oil and 1 fresh green chilli, finely chopped. Leave for 20 minutes before grilling until brown and crisp. Serve 2 slices per person on top of the pilaf.

butter bean & potato casserole

Serves **4**
Preparation time **15 minutes**
Cooking time **1 hour**

olive oil spray
1 mild **Spanish onion**, sliced
2 **garlic cloves**, crushed
200 g (7 oz) **potatoes**, peeled
and diced
65 g (2½ oz) **turnip**, peeled
and thinly sliced
2 x 410 g (13½ oz) cans
butter beans, rinsed and
drained
100 ml (3½ fl oz) **red wine**
400 g (13 oz) can **chopped
tomatoes**
250 ml (8 fl oz) **vegetable
stock**
pinch of **paprika**
1 **bay leaf**
2 tablespoons chopped **flat
leaf parsley**
salt and pepper

Spray a flameproof casserole pan with oil, add the onion and cook over low heat for 10 minutes. Add the garlic, potatoes, turnip and butter beans and stir to combine.

Add all the remaining ingredients, season to taste and bring to a simmer.

Transfer the casserole to in a preheated oven, 180°C (350°), Gas Mark 4, and cook for 45 minutes. Check the seasoning, remove the bay leaf and sprinkle with chopped parsley. Serve with a green salad, if liked.

For butter bean & tomato casserole, omit the potatoes and turnips and instead use 2 sliced onions, 3 x 410 g (13½ oz) cans butter beans and 2 x 400 g (13 oz) chopped tomatoes. Add several sprigs of fresh oregano and simmer on the hob for 15 minutes, rather than in the oven. Serve warm with crusty bread.

vietnamese rolls with peanut dip

Serves **4**
Preparation time **20 minutes**,
  plus soaking
Cooking time **5 minutes**

50 g (2 oz) **rice vermicelli
  noodles**
12 **rice paper rounds**
½ **cucumber**, deseeded
  and shredded
1 **carrot**, shredded
2 **spring onions**, shredded
15 g (½ oz) **mint leaves**,
  left whole
50 g (2 oz) **bean sprouts**
2 **Chinese leaves**, shredded
50 g (2 oz) **cashew nuts**,
  chopped and roasted

Dipping sauce
2 tablespoons **hoisin sauce**
2 tablespoons **chilli sauce**
2 tablespoons natural
  peanuts, chopped
  and roasted
1 **red chilli**, finely chopped

Cook the noodles according to the instructions on the packet. Drain and set aside.

Soak the rice paper rounds in cold water for 3 minutes or until softened. Do not soak for too long or they will fall apart.

Mix together the cucumber, carrot, spring onions, mint, bean sprouts, Chinese leaves and cashew nuts.

Make the sauce by mixing the hoisin and chilli sauces with the peanuts and chilli.

Put a generous spoonful of vegetables in the centre of each rice paper round, roll it up tightly and fold over the ends. Serve the rolls immediately with the dipping sauce.

For chilli & honey dipping sauce, replace the hoisin sauce with 2 tablespoons soy sauce and the chilli sauce with 2 tablespoons honey. Omit the peanuts and combine with 1 finely chopped red chilli.

sweet potato & cheese frittata

Serves **4**
Preparation time **10 minutes**
Cooking time **20 minutes**

500 g (1 lb) **sweet potatoes**, sliced
1 teaspoon **olive oil**
5 **spring onions**, sliced
2 tablespoons chopped **fresh coriander**
4 large **eggs**, beaten
100 g (3½ oz) round **goats' cheese with rind**, cut into 4 slices
pepper

Put the sweet potato slices in a saucepan of boiling water and cook for 7–8 minutes or until just tender, then drain.

Heat the oil in a medium nonstick frying pan, add the spring onions and sweet potato slices and fry for 2 minutes.

Stir the coriander into the beaten eggs, season with plenty of pepper and pour into the pan. Arrange the slices of goats' cheese on top and continue to cook for 3–4 minutes until almost set.

Put the pan under a preheated hot grill and cook for 2–3 minutes until golden and bubbling. Serve immediately, with a green salad if liked.

For butternut squash & feta frittata, replace the sweet potatoes with 500 g (1 lb) cubed butternut squash. Sprinkle feta cheese on top of the frittata in place of the goats' cheese.

roasted vegetable & potato bake

Serves **4**

Preparation time **15 minutes**

Cooking time **45 minutes**

1 tablespoon **olive oil**

200 g (7 oz) **waxy potatoes**, cut into chunks

1 **yellow pepper**, cored, deseeded and roughly diced

2 **red peppers**, cored, deseeded and roughly diced

4 **garlic cloves**, halved

2 tablespoons chopped **thyme**

2 **bay leaves**

125 g (4 oz) **feta cheese**

2 tablespoons chopped **mint**

2 tablespoons chopped **dill**

50 g (2 oz) **extra light cream cheese**

1 **beefsteak tomato**, roughly diced

200 g (7 oz) small **courgettes**, halved lengthways

salt and pepper

Toss the oil with the potatoes, peppers, garlic, thyme and bay leaves in an ovenproof serving dish and cook in a preheated oven, 200°C (400°F), Gas Mark 6, for 30 minutes.

Mash together the feta, mint, dill and cream cheese and season to taste.

Add the tomato and courgettes to the vegetables. Spoon the feta and cream cheese mixture over the vegetables and bake for a further 15 minutes until golden. Garnish with thyme sprigs and serve immediately, with a green salad.

For vegetable crumble, use 75 g (3 oz) rye breadcrumbs, 2 tablespoons chopped fennel and 50 g (2 oz) finely grated Wensleydale cheese and mash together. Spoon over the vegetables and bake as above.

oven-baked ratatouille

Serves **4**
Preparation time **25 minutes**
Cooking time **about 1¼ hours**

1 tablespoon **olive oil**
1 **onion**, chopped
2 **garlic cloves**, finely
  chopped
1 **fennel bulb**, about 250 g
  (8 oz), diced
3 different coloured **peppers**,
  cored, deseeded and diced
2 **courgettes**, about 300 g
  (10 oz) in total, diced
400 g (13 oz) can **chopped
tomatoes**
150 ml (¼ pint) **vegetable
stock**
1 teaspoon **caster sugar**
salt and pepper

Goats' cheese topping
1 **baguette,** about 150 g
  (5 oz), thinly sliced
125 g (4 oz) **goats' cheese
with chives**

Heat the oil over a high heat in a large, nonstick frying pan, add the onion and fry, stirring, for 5 minutes or until lightly browned. Add the garlic and remaining fresh vegetables and fry for a further 2 minutes.

Stir in the tomatoes, stock, sugar and a little seasoning. Bring to the boil, stirring, then transfer to a deep ovenproof dish. Cover the top of the dish with foil and bake in a preheated oven, 190°C (375°F), Gas Mark 5, for 45–60 minutes until the vegetables are tender.

When the vegetables are almost ready, grill one side of the bread slices. Slice the cheese and add one slice to each untoasted side of bread. Remove the foil from the ratatouille, stir the vegetables and top with the toasts, cheese side up.

Put the ratatouille under a preheated hot grill for 4–5 minutes until the cheese is just beginning to melt. Spoon into shallow bowls and serve with a rocket salad.

For herb cobbler, to serve as an accompaniment, make scone dough by sifting together 250 g (8 oz) flour with ½ teaspoon baking powder and combine with 50 g (2 oz) butter and 2 finely chopped spring onions. Add a pinch of dried herbs and bake in a round topped with a little grated mature Cheddar cheese for 20 minutes, while the ratatouille is baking. Cut into wedges and serve with the ratatouille.

asparagus & dolcelatte risotto

Serves **4**
Preparation time **10 minutes**
Cooking time **about 25 minutes**

1 teaspoon **olive oil**
1 small **onion**, finely chopped
300 g (10 oz) **asparagus**, halved and the stem end finely sliced
350 g (12 oz) **risotto rice**
2 tablespoons **dry white wine**
1.2 litres (2 pints) **vegetable stock**
75 g (3 oz) **dolcelatte cheese**, chopped
2 tablespoons chopped **parsley**

Heat the oil in a large, nonstick frying pan, add the onion and sliced asparagus, reserving the tips, and fry for 2–3 minutes until beginning to soften.

Add the rice and coat in the oil, then add the wine and allow it to be absorbed.

Bring the stock to the boil and add it to the rice mixture, ladle by ladle, allowing the liquid to be absorbed before adding any more. With the last addition of stock (which should be about 20 minutes from when you started), add the asparagus tips.

Once all the stock has been absorbed, gently stir through the remaining ingredients and, if liked, serve the risotto with a rocket and tomato salad.

For rocket risotto, quickly fry the onion and cook 300 g (10 oz) risotto rice in 1.2 litres (2 pints) stock as above, then stir in 50 g (2 oz) torn rocket leaves when the rice is cooked. Use whole leaves to garnish.

salads

thai noodle salad

Serves **4**
Preparation time **15 minutes**,
  plus cooling
Cooking time **5 minutes**

200 g (7 oz) **flat rice noodles**
1 tablespoon **sesame oil**
125 g (4 oz) **pork fillet**, diced
1 tablespoon **light soy sauce**
1 tablespoon **sesame seeds**,
  toasted
2 **shallots**, peeled and
  chopped
12 **baby sweetcorn**, chopped
75 g (3 oz) **bean sprouts**
75 g (3 oz) **peanuts**, chopped
  and toasted
4 tablespoons chopped **fresh
  coriander**

Lime and coconut dressing
2 **garlic cloves**, crushed
2 tablespoons **lime juice**
½ **lemon grass** stalk, finely
  chopped
½ **red chilli**, chopped
125 ml (4 fl oz) **reduced-fat
  coconut milk**
1 tablespoon **Thai fish sauce**
salt

Cook the noodles according to the instructions on the packet. Drain.

Meanwhile, heat the sesame oil in a frying pan and gently fry the diced pork for 1–2 minutes. Stir in the soy sauce and cook for 1–2 minutes or until the pork is sticky and coated. Set aside to cool.

Stir the sesame seeds, shallots, sweetcorn and bean sprouts into the cold pork.

Make the dressing by mixing together all the ingredients in a bowl.

Stir the dressing through the noodles and pork, add the peanuts and coriander and serve immediately.

For rice & prawn salad, cook 250 g (8 oz) rice according to the packet instructions. Replace the pork with 350 g (11½ oz) peeled, cooked prawns. Rather than frying the prawns, simply stir them through the soy sauce.

puy lentil & goats' cheese salad

Serves **4**
Preparation time **10 minutes**
Cooking time **about 30 minutes**

2 teaspoons **olive oil**
2 teaspoons **cumin seeds**
2 **garlic cloves**, crushed
2 teaspoons grated **fresh root ginger**
125 g (4 oz) **Puy lentils**
750 ml (1¼ pints) **vegetable stock**
2 tablespoons chopped **mint**
2 tablespoons chopped **fresh coriander**
½ **lime**
150 g (5 oz) **baby spinach** leaves
125 g (4 oz) **goats' cheese**
pepper

Heat the oil in a saucepan over medium heat, add the cumin seeds, garlic and ginger and cook for 1 minute. Add the lentils and cook for a further minute.

Add the stock to the pan, stir and simmer for 25 minutes, until all the liquid is absorbed and the lentils are tender. Check the seasoning. Remove the pan from the heat and set aside to cool. Stir in the mint and coriander and add a squeeze of lime.

Arrange the spinach leaves in individual bowls, top with a quarter of the lentils and the goats' cheese and serve sprinkled with black pepper.

For lentil & egg salad, replace the cheese with 4 hard-boiled eggs, quartered. Make the salad as above and sprinkle with 50 g (2 oz) chopped green olives and the eggs.

trout & cracked wheat salad

Serves **4**
Preparation time **10 minutes**,
 plus cooling
Cooking time **20 minutes**

400 g (13 oz) **cracked wheat**
1 tablespoon **olive oil**
375 g (12 oz) **smoked trout
 fillet**, flaked
1 **cucumber**, deseeded and
 diced
150 g (5 oz) **baby spinach
 leaves**, washed
1 **red onion**, sliced
200 g (7 oz) can **green
 lentils**, rinsed and drained
75 g (3 oz) **sugar snap peas**,
 finely sliced

**Lemon and poppy seed
 dressing**
grated rind of 2 **lemons**
4 tablespoons **lemon juice**
2 tablespoons **poppy seeds**
2 tablespoons chopped **dill**
salt and pepper

Cook the cracked wheat according to the instructions on the packet. Stir through the oil and set aside.

Stir the trout into the cooled cracked wheat, then add the cucumber, spinach, red onion, lentils and peas.

Make the dressing by mixing together the lemon rind and juice, poppy seeds and dill. Season the dressing to taste and just before serving drizzle it over the salad.

For smoked mackerel salad, use 375 g (12 oz) smoked mackerel instead of the smoked trout. Serve with a horseradish dressing instead of the lemon and poppy seed, combining 2 tablespoons creamed horseradish with 4 tablespoons mild yogurt.

chicken, pineapple & rice salad

Serves **4**
Preparation time **40 minutes**

4 boneless, skinless **chicken
    breasts**, about 125 g (4 oz)
    each, cooked
200 g (7 oz) **wholegrain rice**,
    cooked
½ **pineapple**, chopped
1 **red pepper**, chopped
3 **spring onions**, chopped
50 g (2 oz) **dried blueberries**
salt and pepper

Mustard dressing
3 tablespoons **sunflower oil**
4 tablespoons **Dijon mustard**
1 tablespoon **red
    wine vinegar**

Dice the chicken and put it in a large bowl with the
rice. Stir in the pineapple, red pepper, spring onions
and blueberries. Season to taste with salt and pepper.

Make the dressing by mixing all the ingredients with
2 tablespoons water. Season to taste.

Spoon the dressing over the chicken mixture and
serve straightaway.

For walnut, flageolet bean & blueberry rice salad,
replace the pineapple and dried blueberries with
150 g (5 oz) fresh blueberries and add 75 g (3 oz)
fresh walnut halves and a 410 g (13½ oz) can canned
flageolet beans, drained and rinsed. Mix together and
season as above.

bean, kabanos & pepper salad

Serves **4**
Preparation time **10 minutes**,
   plus cooling
Cooking time **20 minutes**

3 **red peppers**, cored and
   deseeded
1 **red chilli**, deseeded and
   sliced
1 tablespoon **olive oil**
1 **onion**, sliced
75 g (3 oz) **kabanos
   sausage**, thinly sliced
2 x 410 g (13½ oz) cans
   butter or **flageolet beans**,
   rinsed and drained
1 tablespoon **balsamic
   vinegar**
2 tablespoons chopped **fresh
   coriander**

Put the peppers on a baking sheet, skin side up, and cook under a preheated hot grill for 8—10 minutes until the skins are blackened. Cover with damp kitchen paper. When the peppers are cool enough to handle, remove the skins and slice the flesh.

Heat the oil in a nonstick frying pan, add the onion and fry for 5—6 minutes until soft. Add the kabanos sausage and fry for 1—2 minutes until crisp.

Mix together the beans and balsamic vinegar, then add the onion and kabanos mixture and the peppers and chilli. Serve the salad with walnut bread, if liked.

For bean, pepper & olive salad with haloumi, omit the kabanos sausage and mix 50 g (2 oz) halved pitted black olives with the beans. Slice and grill 75 g (3 oz) haloumi. Divide the salad among bowls and top with the haloumi.

Italian grilled chicken salad

Serves **4**

Preparation time **20 minutes**, plus cooling

Cooking time **about 15 minutes**

4 **chicken breasts**, about 125 g (4 oz) each
8 small **plum tomatoes**, halved
olive oil spray
400 g (13 oz) **new potatoes**
75 g (3 oz) **baby spinach leaves**
salt and pepper

Italian dressing
10 **basil leaves**, chopped
2 tablespoons chopped **oregano**
1 **garlic clove**, chopped
1 tablespoon **olive oil**
2 tablespoons **lemon juice**
1 tablespoons **Dijon mustard**
grated rind of 1 **lemon**

Use a sharp knife to cut each chicken breast in half horizontally. Arrange the 8 pieces of chicken on a foil-lined grill pan with the tomatoes. Season and spray with oil.

Cook the chicken under a preheated hot grill for about 2 minutes or until it is just cooked and still succulent. Set aside to cool, then cut the chicken into bite-sized pieces.

Meanwhile, steam or boil the potatoes. Set aside to cool, then slice into rounds.

Make the dressing by mixing together all the ingredients.

Combine the chicken, spinach, tomatoes and potatoes in a serving dish. Just before serving, pour over the dressing.

For Italian vegetable salad, omit the chicken and boil 200 g (7 oz) trimmed fine green beans for 3 minutes. Toast 2 tablespoons pine nuts briefly in the oven. Prepare the salad as above, combining the beans with the other ingredients. Toss with the Italian dressing and serve topped with the pine nuts and shavings of Parmesan cheese.

red roasted pork & quinoa salad

Serves **4**

Preparation time **10 minutes**,
plus cooling

Cooking time **15 minutes**

1 tablespoon **sunflower oil**

2 **star anise**

1 tablespoon **demerara sugar**

1 tablespoon **five spice
powder**

1 tablespoon **soy sauce**

1 tablespoon **paprika**

500 g (1 lb) **pork fillet**, thinly
sliced

300 g (10 oz) **quinoa**

200 g (7 oz) **sugar snap
peas**, halved

4 **spring onions**, chopped

1 head of **Chinese leaves**,
shredded

dill sprigs (optional)

Yogurt dressing

125 ml (4 fl oz) **Greek yogurt**

2 tablespoons **water**

2 tablespoons chopped **dill**

salt and pepper

Mix together the oil, star anise, sugar, five spice powder, soy sauce and paprika. Add the pork and stir to coat, then transfer to a roasting tin. Cover and cook in a preheated oven, 180°C (350°F), Gas Mark 4, for 15 minutes or until just cooked but not dry. Remove, uncover and set aside to cool.

Meanwhile, cook the quinoa according to the instructions on the packet. Set aside to cool.

Toss the quinoa with the peas, spring onion and Chinese leaves. Add the pork and the cooking juices, if liked.

Make the dressing by mixing together all the ingredients. Season to taste, drizzle the dressing over the salad and serve sprinkled with dill sprigs, if liked.

For tandoori spiced pork, mix 2 tablespoons tandoori spice with 100 ml (3½ fl oz) yogurt, pour over the pork fillet and roast as above. For a raita style dressing to accompany the pork, use ½ white sliced cabbage mixed with 300 ml (½ pint) yogurt and 1 grated carrot. Add 1 tablespoon roasted cumin seeds to the dressing and mix well.

italian broccoli & egg salad

Serves **4**
Preparation time **10 minutes**
Cooking time **8 minutes**

300 g (10 oz) **broccoli**
2 small **leeks**, about 300 g
  (10 oz) in total, trimmed, slit
  and well rinsed
4 tablespoons **lemon juice**
2 tablespoons **olive oil**
2 teaspoons **clear honey**
1 tablespoon **capers**, well
  drained
2 tablespoons chopped
  tarragon
4 hard-boiled **eggs**
salt and pepper

Cut the broccoli into florets and thickly slice the stems and the leeks. Put the broccoli in the top of a steamer, cook for 3 minutes, add the leeks and cook for another 2 minutes.

Mix together the lemon juice, oil, honey, capers and tarragon in a salad bowl and season to taste.

Shell and roughly chop the eggs.

Add the broccoli and leeks to the dressing, toss together and sprinkle with the chopped eggs. Garnish with tarragon sprigs, if liked, and serve warm with extra thickly sliced wholemeal bread.

For broccoli, cauliflower & egg salad, use 150 g (5 oz) broccoli and 150 g (5 oz) cauliflower instead of 300 g (10 oz) broccoli. Cut the cauliflower into small florets and steam with the broccoli. Serve with a blue cheese dressing made by mixing together 75 g (3 oz) blue cheese, 6 chopped sun-dried tomatoes and 3 tablespoons balsamic vinegar.

turkey skewers & bulgar salad

Serves **4**
Preparation time **10 minutes**,
  plus marinating
Cooking time **20 minutes**

2 tablespoons **sunflower oil**
2 tablespoons **lemon juice**
1 teaspoon **paprika**
3 tablespoons chopped **flat
  leaf parsley**, plus extra to
  garnish
400 g (13 oz) **turkey breast**,
  diced
salt and pepper

Bulgar salad
400 ml (14 fl oz) **chicken
  stock**
250 g (8 oz) **bulgar wheat**
410 g (13½ oz) can **green
  lentils**, rinsed and drained
½ **cucumber**
10 **cherry tomatoes**
20 g (¾ oz) **mint**, chopped
lemon wedges, to garnish

Hummus dressing
4 tablespoons **hummus**
1 tablespoon **lemon juice**

Presoak 8 wooden skewers in warm water. Mix together the oil, lemon juice, paprika and parsley, and season to taste. Add the turkey and turn to coat thoroughly. Set aside for at least 20 minutes.

Drain the turkey (discard any marinade) and thread the pieces on to the skewers. Cook under a preheated hot grill, turning once or twice, for 10 minutes or until cooked through.

Meanwhile, bring the stock to the boil and cook the bulgar wheat according to the instructions on the packet. Drain and spread out to cool. Stir in the green lentils, cucumber, tomatoes and mint.

Make the dressing by combining the hummus with the lemon juice and 1 tablespoon water.

Serve the turkey skewers with the bulgar wheat salad, garnished with lemon wedges and flat leaf parsley. Offer the dressing separately.

For pasta shapes salad, instead of the bulgar salad, replace the lentils and bulgar wheat with 250 g (8 oz) cooked small pasta shapes. Instead of the hummus dressing, mix together 200 ml (7 fl oz) fromage frais with 10 g (1 oz) each chopped fresh basil and mint.

spiced orange & avocado salad

Serves **4**
Preparation time **10 minutes**

4 large juicy **oranges**
2 small ripe **avocados**, peeled
and stoned
2 teaspoons **cardamom pods**
3 tablespoons **light olive oil**
1 tablespoon **clear honey**
generous pinch of **ground
allspice**
2 teaspoons **lemon juice**
salt and pepper
watercress sprigs, to garnish

Cut the skin and the white membrane off the oranges.
Working over a bowl to catch the juice, cut between
the membranes to remove the segments.

Slice the avocados and toss gently with the orange
segments. Pile on to serving plates.

Reserve a few whole cardamom pods for decoration.
Crush the remaining pods to extract the seeds and
pick out and discard the pods. Mix the seeds with the
oil, honey, allspice, lemon juice, salt and pepper and
reserved orange juice.

Garnish with watercress, spoon the dressing over the
top and serve.

For grapefruit & avocado salad, replace the oranges
with 2 large grapefruits and add 100 g (3½ oz)
blueberries. Replace the ground allspice with
1 teaspoon nutmeg.

chilli beef salad with coriander

Serves **4**
Preparation time **20 minutes**
Cooking time **10 minutes**

400 g (13 oz) **beef rump
steaks**
4 **wheat tortillas**, cut into
8 wedges
75 g (3 oz) **baby spinach
leaves**, washed
salt and pepper

Lime and coriander dressing
15 g (½ oz) **fresh coriander
leaves**
2 tablespoons **lime juice**
1 tablespoon **sunflower oil**
1 **garlic clove**, crushed
1 **red chilli**, finely chopped

Season the beef. Heat a large frying pan and sear the beef over high heat until it is cooked but still pink. This will take about 2 minutes each side, depending on thickness. Set aside at room temperature.

Grill the tortillas under a preheated hot grill for about 5 minutes, shaking the pan frequently, until they are crispy. Set aside to cool.

Meanwhile, make the dressing by combining all the ingredients.

Thinly slice the beef and arrange it on the spinach leaves. Spoon over the dressing just before serving with the tortilla wedges.

For crushed new potatoes with coriander dressing, to serve as an accompaniment, boil 750 g (1½ lb) new potatoes for 12 minutes until soft. Crush, not mash, the potatoes and serve drizzled with the coriander dressing and a handful of pine nuts.

herby butter bean salad

Serves **4**
Preparation time **10 minutes**

720 g (1½ lb) jar *judion de la
granja beans* or **butter
beans**, rinsed and drained
25 g (1 oz) **Serrano ham**,
chopped
4 ripe **tomatoes**, sliced
1 mild **Spanish onion**, sliced

Herb dressing
20 g (¾ oz) chopped **flat leaf
parsley**
20 g (¾ oz) chopped **mint**
grated rind and juice of
2 lemons
2 **garlic cloves**, crushed
1 tablespoon **olive oil**
2 teaspoons **cider vinegar**
1 teaspoon chopped
anchovies (optional)
salt and pepper

Arrange the beans and ham in a serving dish with the
sliced tomatoes and onion.

Make the dressing by mixing together the parsley, mint,
lemon rind and juice, garlic, oil and vinegar. Season to
taste and stir in the anchovies, if using.

Drizzle the dressing over the beans and ham and serve.

For herby chickpea & tuna salad, use 2 x 410 g
(13½ oz) cans chickpeas and a 180 g (6½ oz) can
tuna instead of the butter beans and ham. Drain the
chickpeas and tuna and toss together, then add the
tomatoes and onion and divide among serving dishes.
Mix the dressing and pour over the salad. Serve with
slices of ciabatta.

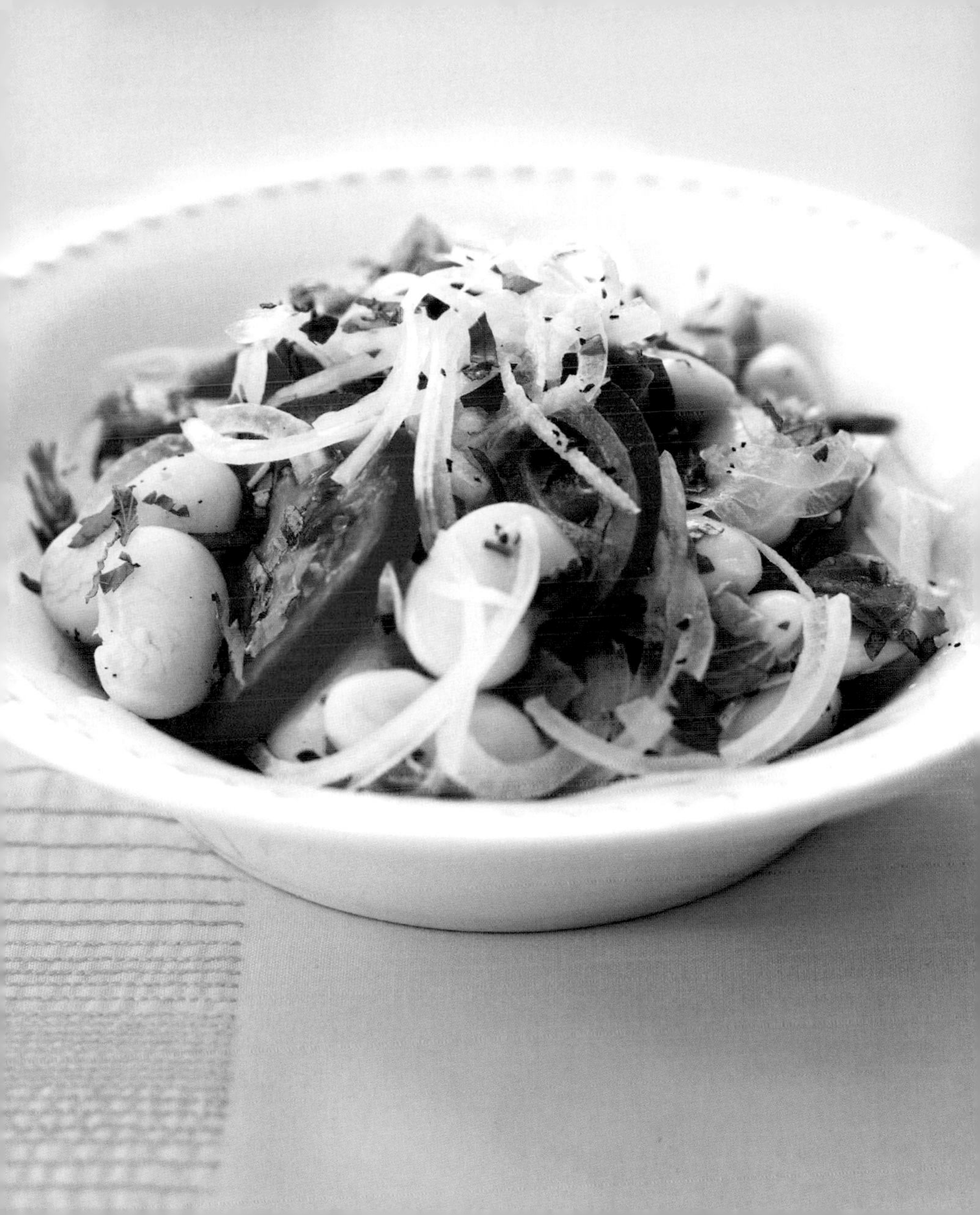

salmon & quails' egg salad

Serves **4**
Preparation time **15 minutes**
Cooking time **3–6 minutes**

12 **quails' eggs**
200 g (7 oz) baby **asparagus**,
   ends trimmed
1 red **oak-leaf lettuce**
1 head **curly endive**
250 g (8 oz) **smoked salmon**
juice of 1 **lime**
salt and pepper
a few **chervil** sprigs, to
   garnish

Lemon dressing
grated rind and juice of
   2 **unwaxed lemons**
½ teaspoon **English mustard**
1 **egg yolk**
9 dessertspoons **olive oil**

Boil the eggs for 3 minutes, then drain and cool them under cold running water. Peel the eggs and place in salted water and set aside until required.

Meanwhile, put the asparagus in a pan of boiling water and cook over a medium heat for 3–5 minutes or until tender. Drain, refresh under cold running water and set aside.

Make the dressing by putting the lemon rind and juice, mustard and egg yolk in a food processor or blender. Process briefly to combine the ingredients thoroughly, then, on a low speed, add the oil in a steady stream. Season to taste.

Separate the lettuce and endive leaves, removing any tough stalks, and wash thoroughly. Put the leaves in a bowl and add two-thirds of the dressing. Toss to distribute the dressing evenly, then arrange in the centre of 4 serving plates.

Divide the salmon into 4 and arrange it on the salad leaves. Sprinkle with lime juice. Halve the eggs and arrange them over the salad. Drizzle with the remaining dressing, garnish with chervil sprigs and serve.

For trout & egg salad, use 4 hens' eggs instead of the quails' eggs, boiling them for about 10 minutes. Replace the smoked salmon with the same quantity of smoked trout fillets. Skin the trout and flake the flesh, discarding any bones. Sprinkle the trout over the leaves, then quarter the eggs and arrange on top.

squid salad with greek potatoes

Serves **4**
Preparation time **30 minutes**
Cooking time **2 minutes**

500 g (1 lb) prepared **squid**
2 tablespoons **lemon juice**
2 tablespoons **olive oil**
1 **garlic clove**, chopped
2 tablespoons chopped **flat
  leaf parsley**
500 g (1 lb) **new potatoes**,
  cooked
200 g (7 oz) **cherry
  tomatoes**, halved
4 **spring onions**, chopped
salt and pepper
lemon wedges, to serve

Cut the squid bodies in half widthways, then in half again so that they open out into squares. Score on one side and mix with the lemon juice and some seasoning.

Cook the squid in a preheated heavy-based frying pan or griddle pan over high heat for 1 minute on each side. Stir in the oil, garlic and parsley, then remove from the heat and set aside to cool.

Spoon the squid and dressing over the potatoes, tomatoes and spring onions and serve with some lemon wedges.

For prawn salad with green olives, use 500 g (1 lb) peeled raw tiger prawns with shells on instead of the squid. Defrost if frozen and rinse under cold water. Season and mix with the lemon juice. Cook on a griddle pan as for the squid, then finish as above, adding 50 g (2 oz) sliced pitted green olives to the cooked prawns. Sprinkle with grated lemon rind before serving.

crab & grapefruit salad

Serves **4**
Preparation time **10 minutes**

400 g (13 oz) **white crab meat**
1 **pink grapefruit**, peeled and sliced
50 g (2 oz) **rocket**
3 **spring onions**, sliced
200 g (7 oz) **mangetout**, halved
salt and pepper

Watercress dressing
85 g (3¼ oz) **watercress**, tough stalks removed
1 tablespoon **Dijon mustard**
2 tablespoon **olive oil**

To serve
4 **chapattis**
lime wedges

Combine the crab meat, grapefruit, rocket, spring onions and mangetout in a serving dish. Season to taste.

Make the dressing by blending together the watercress, mustard and oil. Season with salt.

Toast the chapattis. Stir the dressing into the salad and serve with the toasted chapattis and lime wedges on the side.

For prawn, potato & asparagus salad, substitute 400 g (13 oz) cooked peeled prawns for the crab and 100 g (3½ oz) cooked asparagus for the grapefruit, and add 200 g (7 oz) cooked and cooled potatoes.

spring vegetable salad

Serves **4**
Preparation time **10 minutes**
Cooking time **10 minutes**

200 g (7 oz) fresh or frozen
  peas
200 g (7 oz) **asparagus**,
  trimmed
200 g (7 oz) **sugar snap
  peas**
2 **courgettes**, cut into long,
  thin ribbons
1 **fennel bulb**, thinly sliced
grated rind and juice of
  1 **lemon**
1 teaspoon **Dijon mustard**
1 teaspoon **clear honey**
1 tablespoon chopped **flat
  leaf parsley**
2 tablespoons **olive oil**

Garlic bread
4 **ciabatta rolls**, halved
1 **garlic clove**

Put the peas, asparagus and sugar snap peas in a
saucepan of salted boiling water and simmer for 3
minutes. Drain, then refresh under cold running water.

Transfer the vegetables to a large bowl with the
courgette ribbons and fennel and mix together.

Whisk together the lemon rind and juice, mustard,
honey, parsley and half the oil in a separate bowl.
Toss this dressing through the vegetables.

Rub the cut sides of the rolls with the garlic clove,
drizzle over the remaining oil, then place the rolls on
a baking sheet under a preheated hot grill and toast on
both sides. Serve with the salad.

For poached eggs on spicy toasts, remove
the crusts from 4 slices multigrain bread. Use
1 tablespoon chilli-infused oil to brush each side of
the bread and grill as above. Poach 4 eggs in a pan
of simmering water with 1 teaspoon vinegar added.
Drain, trim and serve on the toasts, with the salad.

prawn, pea shoot & quinoa salad

Serves **4**
Preparation time **10 minutes**
Cooking time **10 minutes**

300 g (10 oz) **quinoa**
75 g (3 oz) **mangetout**,
 blanched and halved
200 g (7 oz) **asparagus**
 spears, cooked, cooled and
 cut into bite-sized pieces
50 g (2 oz) **pea shoots**
400 g (13 oz) cooked **tiger**
 prawns, shells removed
salt and pepper

Fruit and nut dressing
2 tablespoons **olive oil**
2 tablespoons **lemon juice**
20 g (¾ oz) **dried cranberries**
50 g (2 oz) **hazelnuts**,
 chopped and toasted

Cook the quinoa according to the instructions on the packet. Set aside to cool.

Stir the mangetout and asparagus through the quinoa.

Make the dressing by mixing together the oil, lemon juice, cranberries and hazelnuts.

Spoon the pea shoots and prawns over the quinoa, drizzle over the dressing and serve.

For prawn, bulgar wheat & nut salad, use 300 g (10 oz) bulgar wheat instead of the quinoa. For a nuttier dressing, toast 25 g (1 oz) flaked almonds in a dry pan with the hazelnuts, then mix with the olive oil and the rind and juice of 1 orange.

smoked chicken & onion salad

Serves **4**
Preparation time **10 minutes**

300 g (10 oz) skinless
   smoked chicken breast
2 **red onions**, finely sliced
150 g (5 oz) **cherry**
   tomatoes, halved
50 g (2 oz) **pumpkin seeds**,
   roasted
75 g (3 oz) **mixed salad**
   leaves
salt and pepper

Avocado dressing
1 **avocado**, peeled and diced
2 tablespoons **lime juice**
1 tablespoon of **Dijon**
   mustard

Dice or shred the smoked chicken. Rinse the red onions in water.

Make the dressing by blending together the avocado, lime juice, mustard and seasoning.

Toss together the chicken, onion, tomatoes, pumpkin seeds and salad leaves, drizzle over the dressing and serve.

For smoked chicken, broccoli & pasta salad, cook 250 g (8 oz) rigatoni in boiling salted water for about 12 minutes, until tender. Add 250 g (8 oz) broccoli broken into tiny florets for the final 3 minutes cooking. The broccoli should be very lightly cooked. Drain well and rinse under cold water. Drain again. Prepare the salad as above, without tossing in the leaves. Toss the pasta and broccoli with the chicken mixture. Arrange the leaves in bowls and top with the pasta salad.

desserts

mango & passion fruit trifle

Serves **4**

Preparation time **10 minutes**, plus chilling

4 **sponge fingers**

150 g (5 oz) **fat-free Greek yogurt**

200 g (7 oz) **half-fat crème fraîche**

4 **passion fruit**

1 **mango**, peeled, stoned and diced

Break each biscuit into 4 pieces and arrange them in 4 tumblers.

Mix together the yogurt and crème fraîche. Remove the seedy pulp from the passion fruit and set aside.

Spoon a little passion fruit pulp over the biscuits and then add about half of the mango pieces.

Pour about half the crème fraîche mix over the fruit and top with the remaining mango.

Top with the remaining crème fraîche mix and arrange the rest of the passion fruit on top. Refrigerate for up to 1 hour or serve immediately.

For pineapple & strawberry trifle, replace the mango with 400 g (13 oz) peeled, diced pineapple and replace the passion fruit with 125 g (4 oz) halved strawberries. You can also use any of the wide range of frozen fruit available, but make sure the fruit is fully thawed first. Continue as above.

st clement's cheesecake

Serves **10**
Preparation time **10 minutes**,
 plus cooling and chilling
Cooking time **50 minutes**

50 g (2 oz) **unsalted butter**
175 g (6 oz) **low-fat oat
 biscuits**, crushed
2 x 250 g (8 oz) tubs **quark**
125 g (4 oz) **caster sugar**
2 **eggs**
grated rind and juice of
 2 **oranges**
grated rind and juice of
 1 **lemon**
75 g (3 oz) **sultanas**
juliennes of **orange and
 lemon rind**, to decorate

Lightly grease a 20 cm (8 inch) nonstick, loose-based round cake tin.

Melt the butter in a saucepan, stir in the biscuit crumbs, then press them over the base and side of the cake tin. Bake in a preheated oven, 150°C (300°F), Gas Mark 2, for 10 minutes.

Beat together the remaining ingredients in a bowl, spoon the mixture into the cake tin and bake for 40 minutes until just firm. Turn off the oven and leave the cheesecake to cool in the oven for an hour.

Transfer the cheesecake to the refrigerator for 2 hours, then serve decorated with juliennes of orange and lemon rind.

For lime & raspberry cheesecake, replace the oranges, lemon and sultanas with 2–3 drops vanilla extract and the grated rind and juice of 1 lime, then cook as above. Once chilled, decorate with 125 g (4 oz) raspberries.

passion fruit panna cotta

Serves **4**
Preparation time **20 minutes**, plus setting

2 **gelatine leaves**
8 **passion fruit**
200 g (7 oz) **half-fat crème fraîche**
125 g (4 oz) **fat-free Greek yogurt**
1 teaspoon **caster sugar**
vanilla pod, split

Soften the gelatine leaves in cold water. Halve the passion fruit and remove the seeds, working over a bowl to catch as much juice as you can. Reserve the seeds for decoration.

Combine the crème fraîche, yogurt and passion fruit juice.

Put 100 ml (3½ fl oz) water in a small saucepan, add the sugar and the seeds from the vanilla pod and heat gently, stirring until the sugar has dissolved. Drain the gelatine and add to the pan. Stir until dissolved, then leave to cool to room temperature.

Mix the gelatine mixture into the crème fraîche, then pour into 4 ramekins or moulds. Refrigerate for 6 hours or until set.

Turn the panna cotta out of their moulds by briefly immersing each ramekin in very hot water. Spoon over the reserved seeds to decorate.

For coffee panna cotta, substitute 2 teaspoons strong coffee for the passion fruit and continue as for the recipe, using the vanilla pod. Decorate each panna cotta with chocolate coffee beans, if you like.

raspberry shortbread mess

Serves **4**
Preparation time **5 minutes**

300 g (10 oz) **raspberries**,
  roughly chopped
4 **shortbread fingers**, roughly
  crushed
400 g (13 oz) **low-fat
  fromage frais**
2 tablespoons **icing sugar** or
  artificial sweetener

Reserving a few raspberries for decoration, combine all the ingredients in a bowl. Spoon into 4 serving dishes.

Serve immediately, decorated with the reserved raspberries.

For Eton mess, use 4 meringue nests and 300 g (10 oz) strawberries. Hull and halve or quarter the strawberries, then add them to the fromage frais with the sugar or sweetener. Break the meringues into chunks and fold them through the fromage frais, then pile into glasses and serve.

mango & passion fruit brûlée

Serves **4**

Preparation time **10 minutes**, plus chilling

Cooking time **2 minutes**

1 small **mango**, peeled, stoned and thinly sliced

2 **passion fruit**, flesh scooped out

300 g (10 oz) **low-fat natural yogurt**

200 g (7 oz) **low-fat crème fraîche**

1 tablespoon **icing sugar**

few drops **vanilla extract**

2 tablespoons **demerara sugar**

Arrange the mango slices in 4 ramekins.

Stir together the passion fruit flesh, yogurt, crème fraîche, icing sugar and vanilla extract in a bowl, then spoon the mixture over the mango. Tap each ramekin to level the surface.

Sprinkle over the demerara sugar and cook the brûlées under a preheated hot grill for 1–2 minutes until the sugar has melted. Chill for about 30 minutes, then serve.

For plum & peach brûlée, replace the mango with 2 sliced peaches. Continue as above, replacing the passion fruit with 4 firm but ripe chopped plums. Before grilling, top each ramekin with a piece of chopped crystallized ginger.

blueberry & lemon ice cream

Serves **4**

Preparation time **10 minutes**, plus freezing

500 g (1 lb) frozen **blueberries**

500 g (1 lb) **fat-free Greek yogurt**

125 g (4 oz) **icing sugar**, plus extra to decorate

grated rind of 2 **lemons**

1 tablespoon **lemon juice**

Reserve a few blueberries for decoration. Put the remainder of the blueberries in a food processor or blender with the yogurt, icing sugar and lemon rind and juice and process until smooth.

Spoon the mixture into a 600 ml (1 pint) freezerproof container and freeze.

Eat when the frozen yogurt is softly frozen and easily spoonable. Before serving, decorate with the reserved blueberries and a sprinkling of icing sugar. Use within 3 days.

For peach & blackcurrant ice cream waffles, lightly toast 4 waffles, then top each with a sliced canned peach and drizzle with honey. Serve with blackcurrant and lemon ice cream. Use 500 g (1 lb) frozen blackcurrants in place of the blueberries. The same quantity of frozen blackberries or raspberries can also be used.

pears with maple syrup biscuits

Serves **4**
Preparation time **20 minutes**
Cooking time **50 minutes**

2 **vanilla pods**, split
3 tablespoons **clear honey**
375 ml (13 fl oz) **sweet white wine**
125 g (4 oz) **caster sugar**
4 hard **pears**, such as Packham or Comice, peeled, cored and halved

Maple syrup biscuits
25 g (1 oz) **reduced-fat sunflower spread**
2 tablespoons **maple syrup**
1 tablespoon **caster sugar**
50 g (2 oz) **plain flour**
1 **egg white**

Combine the vanilla pods, honey, wine, sugar and water in a saucepan large enough to hold all the pears. Heat until the sugar dissolves and then add the pears. Simmer for 30 minutes or until the pears are very tender. Remove the pears from the pan with a slotted spoon and set aside.

Simmer the syrup for about 15 minutes until it has reduced. Set aside with the pears until ready to serve.

Make the biscuits. Beat together the sunflower spread, maple syrup and sugar, then stir in the flour. Beat the egg white until softly peaking, then fold it into the mix.

Drop teaspoonfuls of the mixture on to a lightly greased baking sheet, spacing the biscuits well apart. Bake in a preheated oven, 200°C (400°F), Gas Mark 6, for about 8 minutes until golden. Remove and transfer to a rack to cool.

Decorate the pears with a sliver of vanilla pod and serve with a little syrup drizzled over them and a biscuit on the side.

For vanilla & rosewater peaches, replace the pears with the same quantity of peaches and poach in the syrup as above for about 20 minutes or until tender. Halved peaches will take less time. Remove the peaches and continue to simmer the syrup for about 15 minutes until it has reduced. Add 1–2 tablespoons rosewater, to taste, for a more fragrant syrup. Finish as above.

strawberries & meringue

Serves **4**
Preparation time **15 minutes**
Cooking time **2½ hours**

3 **egg whites**
150 g (5 oz) **light muscovado sugar**
3 teaspoons **cornflour**
1 teaspoon **white vinegar**
1 teaspoon **vanilla extract**
250 g (8 oz) **strawberries**, hulled and sliced

Line 4 tart tins or ramekins with nonstick baking paper. Beat the egg whites until they form stiff peaks, then beat in the sugar, a spoonful at a time, making sure the sugar is incorporated between additions.

Fold in the cornflour, vinegar and vanilla extract.

Spoon the mixture into the tart tins or ramekins and cook in a preheated oven, 120°C (250°F), Gas Mark ½, for 2½ hours.

Place the strawberries in an ovenproof dish and bake with the meringues for the last hour of the cooking time.

Spoon the strawberries and any cooking juices over the meringues to serve.

For baked nectarines with orange meringues, add the grated rind of 1 orange to the meringue with the cornflour. Cut 2 peeled and stoned nectarines into thin slices and place in an ovenproof dish. Sprinkle with 2 tablespoons sugar and 1 tablespoon orange juice, then bake for 45 minutes with the meringues. Serve the fruit on the meringues.

lime & mango sorbet

Serves **4**

Preparation time **10 minutes**, plus freezing

Cooking time **5 minutes**

150 g (5 oz) **caster sugar**
250 ml (8 fl oz) **lime juice**
grated rind of **1 lime**
3 **mangoes**, peeled and stoned
2 **egg whites**

Line a 2 lb (1 kg) loaf tin with clingfilm or nonstick baking paper. Put the sugar in a saucepan, add 250 ml (8 fl oz) water and warm gently until the sugar is dissolved. Remove from the heat and stir in the lime juice and grated rind.

Meanwhile, process the mango flesh to make a smooth purée, reserving four thin slices for the decoration. Stir the purée into the lime syrup and pour the mixture into the loaf tin. Freeze for at least 4 hours or overnight until solid.

Remove the sorbet from the tin and blend or process with the egg whites. Return the mixture to the tin and return to the freezer until firm. Eat within 3 days because the flavour of fresh fruit sorbets deteriorates quickly and this one has raw egg in it. Before serving, decorate each portion of sorbet with a thin slice of mango and serve with a couple of wafer biscuits.

For passion fruit sorbet, omit the mangoes and use 250 ml (8 fl oz) passion fruit juice instead of the lime juice. The passion fruit juice can be bought or scooped from fresh fruit. To prepare fresh fruit, halve and scoop out the pips and pulp into a sieve. Rub all the juice through the sieve, then discard the seeds.

mixed berry chocolate roulade

Serves **4**

Preparation time **20 minutes,**
   plus cooling

Cooking time **15 minutes**

3 large **eggs**
100 g (3½ oz) **caster sugar**
½ teaspoon **chocolate extract**
50 g (2 oz) **plain flour**
25 g (1 oz) **cocoa**, plus extra
   to dust
150 g (5 oz) **half-fat crème
   fraîche**
150 g (5 oz) **fat-free Greek
   yogurt**
25 g (1 oz) **icing sugar**
1 tablespoon **chocolate
   sauce**
200 g (7 oz) **mixed berries**,
   chopped, plus extra to
   decorate

Grease and line a 30 x 20 cm (12 x 8 inch) Swiss roll tin. Whisk together the eggs and sugar until the mixer leaves a trail over the surface. Add the chocolate extract, sift in the flour and cocoa and fold in carefully.

Pour the mixture into the prepared tin. Bake in a preheated oven, 200°C (400°F), Gas Mark 6, for 15 minutes.

Place a clean tea towel on the work surface and put a piece of nonstick baking paper on top. When the sponge is cooked, turn it out on to the baking paper, roll it up carefully and leave to cool.

Mix together the crème fraîche, yogurt, icing sugar and chocolate sauce.

Unroll the roulade and spread the crème fraîche mix over it. Spoon the berries over the crème fraîche and roll up the roulade again. Dust with cocoa and serve immediately, decorated with extra berries.

For strawberry & vanilla roulade, omit the cocoa, increase the plain flour to 75 g (3 oz) and use ½ teaspoon vanilla extract instead of the chocolate extract. Use 200 g (7 oz) strawberries to fill the roulade and serve decorated with extra sliced strawberries, if liked.

frozen fruity yogurt

Serves **4**
Preparation time **15 minutes**,
  plus freezing

300 g (10 oz) fresh or frozen
  raspberries
3 **nectarines**, skinned, stoned
  and chopped
2 tablespoons **icing sugar**
400 ml (14 fl oz) **Greek
  yogurt**
200 ml (7 fl oz) **low-fat
  Greek yogurt**

Put half the raspberries and nectarines in a food processor or blender and process until smooth.

Stir the purée and the rest of the fruit into the remaining ingredients, then transfer to a freezerproof container and freeze for 1 hour. Stir well, then return to the freezer and freeze until solid.

Serve the frozen yogurt in scoops, as you would ice cream. It will keep for up to 1 month in the freezer.

For frozen strawberry yogurt, gently cook 250 g (8 oz) hulled and chopped strawberries in 2 tablespoons red grape juice. Strain and stir the juice into 1 tablespoon crème de cassis, 2 tablespoons icing sugar and 300 ml (½ pint) natural yogurt. Continue as above.

very berry muffins

Makes **12**
Preparation time **15 minutes**
Cooking time **25 minutes**

250 g (8 oz) **plain flour**
4 tablespoons **caster sugar**
1 tablespoon **baking powder**
1 **egg**, beaten
200 ml (7 fl oz) **milk**
50 ml (2 fl oz) **vegetable oil**
200 g (7 oz) **mixed berries**,
   roughly chopped

Mix together all of the ingredients, except the berries, to make a smooth dough. Fold in the berries.

Put nonstick paper cases in a 12-section muffin tin and spoon the mixture into the cases. Bake in a preheated oven, 180°C (350°F), Gas Mark 4, for 25 minutes or until a skewer comes out clean when inserted. Transfer to a wire rack to cool.

For banana & pecan muffins, use 200 g (7 oz) chopped fresh banana instead of the berries, adding 125 g (4 oz) chopped pecan nuts with the bananas. Select firm but ripe bananas. Serve warm, drizzled with maple syrup.

chocolate & nectarine cake

Serves **6**
Preparation time **15 minutes**
Cooking time **45 minutes**

3 **nectarines**
75 g (3 oz) **plain dark chocolate**, chopped
25 g (1 oz) **unsalted butter**
2 **egg yolks**
75 g (3 oz) **caster sugar**
½ teaspoon **chocolate extract**
4 **egg whites**
cocoa powder, for dusting

Line with baking paper and grease a 25 cm (10 inch) cake tin. Put the nectarines in a bowl and pour over boiling water. Leave to stand for 1 minute, then peel off the skins. Halve the nectarines and remove the stones. Drain them well on kitchen paper and arrange, cut side down, in the prepared cake tin.

Put the chocolate and butter in a heatproof bowl and melt together over a pan of simmering water.

Beat together the egg yolks and sugar until the whisk leaves a trail when lifted. The mix should be very pale and quite stiff. Stir in the chocolate and chocolate extract.

Beat the egg whites until softly peaking. Stir a spoonful into the cake mix, then fold in the remainder. Spoon the mixture over the nectarines.

Bake the cake in a preheated oven, 180°C (350°F), Gas Mark 4, for 45 minutes or until a skewer inserted comes out clean. Serve warm or cold, dusted with cocoa powder.

For pear & chocolate soufflé cake, make a syrup by bringing 125 g (4 oz) sugar to the boil in 250 ml (8 fl oz) water. Peel 3 pears and poach them in the syrup for 30 minutes at a gentle simmer. Drain the pears, reserving the syrup, then halve, core and drain well. Use these instead of the nectarines in the cake as described above. Add the grated rind of 1 orange to the syrup and boil for 2 minutes, then serve with the cake.

cherry & cinnamon parfait

Serves **4**
Preparation time **10 minutes**,
  plus freezing
Cooking time **5 minutes**

350 g (11½ oz) jar **morello
  cherries in syrup**
pinch of **ground cinnamon**
½ teaspoon **vanilla extract**
1 tablespoon **caster sugar**
1 **egg yolk**
150 g (5 oz) **half-fat crème
  fraîche**
4 **meringue nests**, broken
  into pieces
fresh cherries, to decorate

Drain the cherries and put 100 ml (3½ fl oz) of the
syrup into a small saucepan. Stir the cinnamon, vanilla
extract and sugar into the syrup and heat for 5 minutes
or until the sugar has dissolved. Set aside to cool.

Stir the egg yolk through the crème fraîche. Add the
drained cherries to the syrup, then mix in the crème
fraîche. Fold the meringue nests carefully through
the mixture.

Transfer to a 300 ml (½ pint) freezerproof container
and freeze for at least 4 hours. Eat within a day when
the parfait will be softly frozen. Decorate with fresh
cherries before serving.

For pineapple parfait, omit the morello cherries and
instead drain and chop a 400 g (13 oz) can sliced
pineapple, adding to the syrup as above. Omit the egg
yolk, and combine the pineapple, syrup and crème
fraîche. Fold through the meringue nests.

ricotta & maple syrup cheesecake

Serves **6**
Preparation time **20 minutes**,
  plus chilling

3 **gelatine** leaves
125 g (4 oz) **reduced-fat
  digestive biscuits**, crushed
50 g (2 oz) **reduced-fat
  sunflower spread**, melted
200 g (7 oz) **cottage cheese**
200 g (7 oz) **ricotta cheese**
2 **egg whites**
25 g (1 oz) **icing sugar**,
  sieved
25 ml (1 fl oz) **lemon juice**
4 tablespoons **maple syrup**

To decorate
2 **oranges**, peeled and sliced
sprigs of **redcurrants**

Line a 20 cm (8 inch) springform tin with nonstick baking paper. Soften the gelatine in cold water.

Mix together the biscuit crumbs and melted sunflower spread and press into the prepared tin. Refrigerate.

Sieve together the cottage cheese and ricotta. Beat the egg whites until stiffly peaking, then beat in the icing sugar until glossy.

Put the lemon juice and 50 ml (2 fl oz) water in a saucepan over a low heat and stir in the gelatine until dissolved. Add to the ricotta mix with the maple syrup, then fold in the egg whites. Pour the mixture over the biscuit base and refrigerate until set.

Decorate with the sliced oranges and sprigs of redcurrants before serving.

For raspberry & ricotta cheesecake with chocolate sauce, stir 250 g (8 oz) raspberries into the pan with the ricotta mix, then make the cheesecake as above. To serve, melt 200 g (7 oz) plain chocolate with 4 tablespoons syrup and drizzle over the cheesecake.

banoffee mousse

Serves **4**
Preparation time **10 minutes**,
  plus setting

2 **gelatine** leaves
3 tablespoons **dulce de leche toffee sauce** or **toffee sauce**
125 g (4 oz) **half-fat crème fraîche**
65 g (2½ oz) **honey-dipped banana chips**, chopped
4 **egg whites**

Soften the gelatine in cold water for 2 minutes.

Put the toffee sauce in a small saucepan over gentle heat and stir in the gelatine until it has dissolved.

Stir the toffee mixture into the crème fraîche and add the dried bananas, reserving a few for decoration.

Meanwhile, beat the egg whites until stiff, then fold through the toffee and banana mixture. Spoon into 4 glasses and decorate with the reserved banana chips and an extra dollop of toffee sauce, if you like.

For banana & hazelnut toffee creams, mash 2 fresh bananas and mix with the toffee sauce and crème fraîche, omitting the gelatine and egg whites. Serve topped with 50 g (2 oz) chopped toasted hazelnuts.

chocolate brownies

Makes **9**
Preparation time **10 minutes**
Cooking time **30 minutes**

125 g (4 oz) **reduced-fat
  sunflower spread**
2 **eggs**
125 g (4 oz) **light soft brown
  sugar**
75 g (3 oz) **self-raising flour**
50 g (2 oz) **cocoa**, sieved,
  plus extra to decorate
50 g (2 oz) **plain dark
  chocolate**, chopped
1 teaspoon **chocolate extract**
salt

Grease and line an 18 cm (7 inch) square deep cake tin.

Beat together the sunflower spread, eggs and sugar. Stir in the flour and cocoa, then add the chocolate and chocolate extract. Stir in 1 teaspoon boiling water and a pinch of salt.

Transfer the mixture to the prepared tin and bake in a preheated oven, 190°C (375°F), Gas Mark 5, for 30 minutes or until a skewer comes out clean when inserted in the centre. Leave to cool in the tin then cut into 9 squares. Dust with a little cocoa powder to serve.

For rum & raisin sauce, to go with the brownies, gently heat 300 ml (½ pint) milk in a saucepan with 2 tablespoons cornflour, 4 tablespoons rum and 4 tablespoons raisins. Add sugar to taste, before pouring the sauce over the cooled brownies.

summer fruit compôte

Serves **2**
Preparation time **5 minutes**,
  plus chilling
Cooking time **5 minutes**

250 g (8 oz) **mixed summer
  fruit**, such as raspberries,
  blueberries and strawberries,
  thawed if frozen
finely grated rind and juice of
  1 large **orange**
1 tablespoon **redcurrant jelly**
250 g (8 oz) **plain soya
  yogurt**, to serve

Put the fruit, orange rind and juice and redcurrant jelly in a large saucepan. Cover and cook gently for 5 minutes or until the juices flow and the fruit is softened.

Remove the pan from the heat and set aside. When the fruit is cool, chill it and serve with soya yogurt.

For rhubarb, orange & ginger compôte, omit the mixed summer fruit and redcurrant jelly and use 1 kg (2 lb) rhubarb cut in 2.5 cm (1 inch) pieces. Dissolve 250 g (8 oz) caster sugar in 150 ml (¼ pint) water, bring to the boil and add the rhubarb. Simmer for about 5 minutes then leave to stand. Stir in the grated rind and juice of 1 orange with 3 tablespoons chopped preserved stem ginger, and chill.

index

234

acknowledgements

Executive editor: Nicky Hill
Editor: Fiona Robertson
Executive art editor: Penny Stock
Designer: Grade
Photographer: Lis Parsons
Food stylist: Alice Hart
Props stylist: Liz Hippisley
Senior production manager: Martin Croshaw

Special photography: © Octopus Publishing
Group Limited/Lis Parsons
Other photography: © Octopus Publishing Group
Limited/Frank Adam 129; /William Lingwood 31,
65, 69, 91, 123, 131, 135, 155, 175, 23; /Lis
Parsons 49, 55, 59, 79, 127, 143, 151, 157, 163,
169, 191, 201, 207, 211, 221; /William Reavell
85, 95, 179; /Gareth Sambidge 17, 45, 101, 117,
125, 185